Math and Literature

Grades 2–3

Math and Literature
Grades 2–3

Marilyn Burns
Stephanie Sheffield

Math Solutions Publications
Sausalito, CA

Math Solutions Publications
A division of
Marilyn Burns Education Associates
150 Gate 5 Road, Suite 101
Sausalito, CA 94965
www.mathsolutions.com

Portions of the present work appeared in a slightly different version in *Math and Literature (K–3), Book One* by Marilyn Burns (© 1992 by Math Solutions Publications) and *Math and Literature (K–3), Book Two* by Stephanie Sheffield (© 1995 by Math Solutions Publications).

Library of Congress Cataloging-in-Publication Data
Burns, Marilyn, 1941–
  Math and literature. Grades 2–3 / Marilyn Burns, Stephanie Sheffield.
     p. cm.
  Includes bibliographical references and index.
   ISBN 0-941355-67-5 (alk. paper)
   1. Mathematics—Study and teaching (Elementary) 2. Children's literature in mathematics education.   I. Sheffield, Stephanie. II. Title.
  QA135.6.B7685 2004
  372.7—dc22   2004014362

Editor: Toby Gordon
Production: Melissa L. Inglis
Cover and interior design: Catherine Hawkes/Cat and Mouse
Composition: Interactive Composition Corporation

Printed in the United States of America on acid-free paper
08 07 06 05 04   ML   1 2 3 4 5

A Message from Marilyn Burns

We at Marilyn Burns Education Associates believe that teaching mathematics well calls for increasing our understanding of the math we teach, seeking greater insight into how children learn mathematics, and refining lessons to best promote children's learning. All of our Math Solutions Professional Development publications and inservice courses have been designed to help teachers achieve these goals.

Our publications include a wide range of choices, from books in our new Teaching Arithmetic and Lessons for Algebraic Thinking series to resources that link math and literacy; from books to help teachers understand mathematics more deeply to children's books that help students develop an appreciation for math while learning basic concepts.

Our inservice programs offer five-day courses, one-day workshops, and series of school-year sessions throughout the country, working in partnership with school districts to help implement and sustain long-term improvement in mathematics instruction in all classrooms.

To find a complete listing of our publications and workshops, please visit our Web site at *www.mathsolutions.com*. Or contact us by calling (800) 868-9092 or sending an e-mail to *info@mathsolutions.com*.

We're eager for your feedback and interested in learning about your particular needs. We look forward to hearing from you.

A DIVISION OF MARILYN BURNS EDUCATION ASSOCIATES

Contents

Acknowledgments

Thanks to those teachers who contributed their expertise by sharing their classroom lessons with us: Rusty Bresser, Laurel Elementary School, Oceanside, California; Mary Petry-Cooper, Dr. Howard School, Champaign, Illinois; Bonnie Tank, Jefferson School, San Francisco, California; Leyani von Rotz, Anna Yates Elementary School, Emeryville, California; and Lynne Zolli, Jefferson School, San Francisco, California.

Thanks to those teachers who allowed our lessons to be taught in their classrooms: Connie Cooper, Brill Elementary School, Houston, Texas; Leo Kostelnick, Bolinas-Stinson Elementary School, Stinson Beach, California; Wisha Rose, Brill Elementary School, Houston, Texas; Ken Taylor, Anna Yates Elementary School, Emeryville, California; Dee Uyeda, Park School, Mill Valley, California; Donna Weltin, Park School, Mill Valley, California; and Sandra Yates, Beneke Elementary School, Houston, Texas.

Introduction

For months before publishing this resource of classroom-tested lessons, I was surrounded by children's books. They were stacked practically up to my ears on my desk and additional piles were all around on the floor. It took some fancy shuffling at times to make space for other things that needed my attention. But I never complained. I love children's books and it was pure pleasure to be immersed in reading them and then teaching, writing, revising, and editing lessons that use them as springboards for teaching children mathematics.

This book is one in our new Math Solutions Publications series for teaching mathematics using children's literature, and I'm pleased to present the complete series:

Math and Literature, Grades K–1
Math and Literature, Grades 2–3
Math and Literature, Grades 4–6, Second Edition
Math and Literature, Grades 6–8
Math and Nonfiction, Grades K–2
Math and Nonfiction, Grades 3–5

More than ten years ago we published my book *Math and Literature (K–3)*. My premise for that book was that children's books can be effective vehicles for motivating children to think and reason mathematically. I searched for books that I knew would stimulate children's imaginations and that also could be used to teach important math concepts and skills.

After that first book's publication, my colleague Stephanie Sheffield began sending me titles of children's books she had discovered and descriptions of the lessons she had taught based on them. Three years after publishing my book, we published Stephanie's *Math and*

Literature (K–3), Book Two. And the following year we published Rusty Bresser's *Math and Literature (Grades 4–6),* a companion to the existing books.

Over the years, some of the children's books we initially included in our resources have, sadly, gone out of print. However, other wonderful titles have emerged. For this new series, we did a thorough review of our three original resources. Stephanie and I collaborated on substantially revising our two K–3 books and reorganizing them into two different books, one for grades K–1 and the other for grades 2–3. Rusty produced a second edition of his book for grades 4–6.

In response to the feedback we received from teachers, we became interested in creating a book that would offer lessons based on children's books for middle school students, and we were fortunate enough to find two wonderful teachers, Jennifer M. Bay-Williams and Sherri L. Martinie, to collaborate on this project. I'm pleased to present their book, *Math and Literature, Grades 6–8.*

The two books that round out our series use children's nonfiction as springboards for lessons. Jamee Petersen created *Math and Nonfiction, Grades K–2,* and Stephanie Sheffield built on her experience with the Math and Literature books to team with her colleague Kathleen Gallagher to write *Math and Nonfiction, Grades 3–5.* Hearing nonfiction books read aloud to them requires children to listen in a different way than usual. With nonfiction, students listen to the facts presented and assimilate that information into what they already know about that particular subject. And rather than reading from cover to cover as with fiction, it sometimes makes more sense to read only a small portion of a nonfiction book and investigate the subject matter presented in that portion. The authors of these Math and Nonfiction books are sensitive to the demands of nonfiction and how to present new information in order to make it accessible to children.

We're still fond of the lessons that were based on children's books that are now out of print, and we know that through libraries, the Internet, and used bookstores, teachers have access to some of those books. Therefore, we've made all of the older lessons that are not included in the new series of books available online at *www. mathsolutions.com.* Please visit our Web site for those lessons and for additional support for teaching math.

I'm pleased and proud to present these new books. It was a joy to work on them, and I'm convinced that you and your students will benefit from the lessons we offer.

MARILYN BURNS
2004

Centipede's 100 Shoes
Taught by Marilyn Burns

Centipede's 100 Shoes, by Tony Ross (2003), is a sweet and silly story about a little centipede who goes to the shoe store to buy one hundred shoes. The next morning, after putting on his shoes, he discovers that he bought too many—he only has forty-two legs! Even so, putting on forty-two socks and lacing forty-two shoes takes far too long, and after just a few days, the centipede decides to sell the shoes to creepy-crawlies with fewer legs. Marilyn Burns read the story to a class of third graders and gave the students the problem of verifying that the centipede had indeed sold all one hundred shoes.

MATERIALS

information about the number of legs on
 spiders, beetles, woodlice, and grasshoppers,
 from books or from Internet sites

At the end of *Centipede's 100 Shoes,* the centipede loads his one hundred shoes and forty-two socks in a wheelbarrow and sells the shoes to five spiders, four beetles, two woodlice, and a grasshopper; sells the socks to the five spiders; and has shoes and socks left over for two worms, each of whom only needs one shoe and one sock. Marilyn planned to pose the problem to the third-grade students of verifying that the little centipede had indeed sold all of his shoes and socks, and she prepared by first researching information about the legs on each of the creatures listed. Some of the children would know how many legs some of the creatures had, but Marilyn compiled information on all of them by searching on the Internet through Google. She also printed photographs or illustrations of centipedes (the number of legs varies but rarely do centipedes have one hundred legs), spiders (all have eight legs), beetles (all have six legs, and Marilyn printed the picture of a ladybug, an example of a beetle, which she knew would be familiar to the children), woodlice (all have fourteen legs), and grasshoppers (with six legs each). Marilyn had the printouts with her when she gathered the children on the rug to read the book aloud.

The children loved the story. They giggled at the beginning, when after the little centipede stubbed a toe and went to his mum to make it better, his mum had to kiss many of the toes before finding the one that was hurt. The next day, the little centipede and his mum went to the shoe store to buy one hundred shoes. The students were surprised when the little centipede put on his shoes the next morning and discovered that he had only forty-two legs! They groaned when, even with only forty-two shoes, it took the little centipede until bedtime to lace them up. When the centipede's aunties knit forty-two socks so that the shoes wouldn't hurt the centipede's feet, Travon said, "Now he'll never get dressed in time to go out." The centipede decided that sleeping in his socks would save time, but his mum wouldn't let him do that, so the following morning, he abandoned the idea of wearing shoes and socks and went off to sell them all.

"That's a good story," Ana said when Marilyn finished reading.

"I think he should have gotten the buckle shoes instead of the lace-up shoes," Julie commented.

"Do centipedes really only have forty-two feet?" Warren asked.

"Don't they have a hundred?" Isaac added.

Marilyn responded, "I always thought that centipedes had one hundred legs, so I went on the Internet to do some research." She showed the children the information she had printed out about centipedes and then read a bit of it to them, including that the number of legs varies among centipedes. "So it's possible for centipedes to have only forty-two legs," she said.

Marilyn then reviewed with the class who bought the shoes and socks. She read, "He sold shoes to five spiders, four beetles, two woodlice, and a grasshopper, with socks for the five spiders, and with enough shoes and socks left for two worms." Then she asked a question: "Do you think he sold all one hundred shoes and forty-two socks, or do you think he might have had some left over?" Most of the children thought that the little centipede probably had some left over.

"I think he sold maybe only sixty-four shoes," Priscilla said.

"Why do you think that?" Marilyn asked.

Priscilla thought a moment, shrugged, and said, "One hundred shoes is a lot of shoes, and I don't think they had enough legs."

"Spiders have eight legs," Antonio offered.

"What are woodlice?" William wanted to know.

Marilyn then showed the children the information she had collected about the other creatures. The children were interested in the facts and the photographs. They were surprised to learn that woodlice have fourteen legs, one on each side of the seven sections of their bodies. Marilyn then wrote on the chalkboard:

5 spiders (8 legs each)
4 beetles (6 legs each)
2 woodlice (14 legs each)
1 grasshopper (6 legs each)
2 worms (1 leg each)

"Your job now is to figure out if the author, Tony Ross, figured correctly and if the little centipede really did sell all one hundred shoes and forty-two socks," she told the students. She wrote on the board:

100 shoes
42 socks

Marilyn continued, "On your paper, show how you figure."

"Can we draw pictures?" Daria asked.

Marilyn responded, "Yes, pictures can help you solve the problem, but I also want you to show how you would solve it with numbers."

"I don't know how to draw woodlice," William said.

"I'll put the computer printouts I made up here on the front table and you can come and look at them when you're ready to draw," Marilyn replied.

No other students had questions or comments, and they went to work. The context of the problem made it accessible to all of the children and they were all able to begin working. However, they used different approaches to solve the problem.

Isaac, for example, used multiplication. He represented the number of shoes for each creature with a multiplication sentence—$5 \times 8 = 40$, $4 \times 6 = 24$, $14 \times 2 = 28$, $6 \times 1 = 6$, and $2 \times 1 = 2$. He wrote the products in a column and added the numbers to get one hundred. Then, to check, he made drawings and counted the legs. Next he tackled figuring out that all forty-two socks had been sold. He wrote: *I counted the legs of the spiders and I got 40 and then I just had to count the two worms and that was two so its 42.* (See Figure 1–1.)

Only a few other students also relied on multiplication. Although the students had been studying multiplication, most of them still relied on addition and wrote addition sentences for each. Dawn, for example, drew a picture of five spiders and wrote underneath *8 + 8 + 8 + 8 + 8*, and then figured out, counting on her fingers, that the eight spiders had forty legs. She continued in this way for the other creatures and then, as Isaac had done, wrote *40, 24, 28, 6,* and *2* in a column and added them, using the standard algorithm.

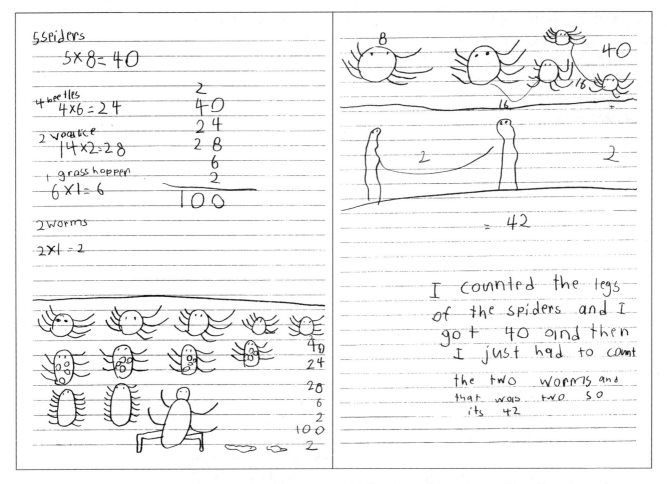

Figure 1–1: Isaac was one of only a few children to rely on multiplication to figure the number of legs for each group of creatures.

Warren did the same, but when he wrote the numbers in a column, he wrote the 6 and the 2 for the grasshopper and the two worms in the tens place, lining them up under the 4 from 40 and the 2s from 24 and 28. "He was wrong," Warren announced. "He should have sold one hundred seventy-two shoes."

Ana, who was sitting next to Warren, looked over at his paper. "Look, you wrote them wrong," she said, pointing to the numbers in the tens column. "See, you have to put the six and the two over here." She pointed to the ones place.

"Oh yeah," Warren said. He erased what he had done and added again. "Now it's a hundred," he said. Warren's error showed the fragility of his understanding of place value.

Other children showed how they figured out the total legs for each group of creatures. For the spiders, for example, Daria knew that two spiders had sixteen legs, so she added sixteen and sixteen to figure out that four spiders had thirty-two legs, and then added eight to thirty-two to get forty. She worked carefully and methodically to verify that the centipede had sold all of the shoes and socks. She wrote on her paper: *Was tony ross right yes!* (See Figure 1–2.)

On her paper, Juanita wrote a long column of numbers—five 8s, four 6s, two 14s, then 6, and finally, two 1s. Juanita's understanding of place value was weak and she generally relied on counting by ones. She added the first two 8s to get sixteen, then counted on eight more to get twenty-four, then eight more to get thirty-two, each time writing the new sum to the right of the column of numbers. When Marilyn stopped by her desk, she had just added six onto forty to get forty-six. While Juanita's method could have led to the right answer, the chance of making an error along the way was likely, and Marilyn worried that she would become frustrated. Also, she wanted to see if she could help Juanita with a more efficient strategy that would involve thinking about tens and ones. Marilyn sat down and talked with her.

"Do you know how many shoes the five spiders bought?" she asked, curious if Juanita would relate the 40 she had written on her paper to the problem. She did.

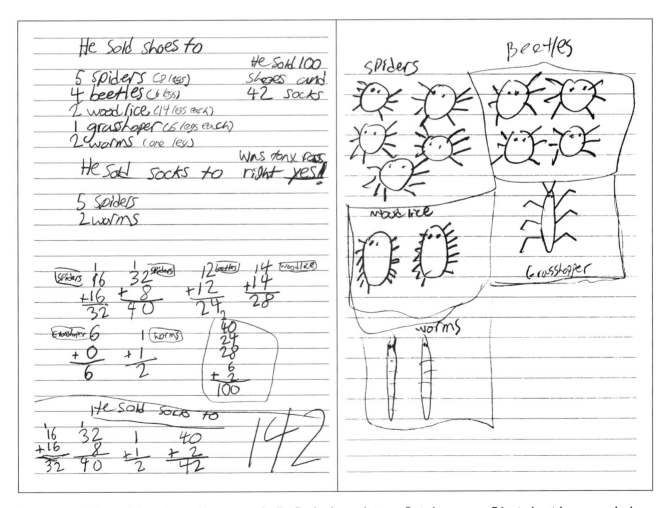

Figure 1–2: After solving the problem numerically, Daria drew pictures. But she was confident about her numerical work and didn't use the pictures to verify her answers.

"Forty," Juanita said. "I added eight and eight and eight and eight and eight, and I got forty. Now I'm adding the sixes."

"Now that you know about the spiders, how about writing the forty down and then starting over with the sixes to figure out how many shoes the beetles bought?" Marilyn suggested. "Then you can add them up at the end." Juanita was a methodical child, and Marilyn's suggestion made sense to her. After a while, however, she came to Marilyn for help. She had listed four numbers and what they each represented—40, 24, 28, and 8. (The 8 was for the number of legs for the grasshopper and the two worms combined.) Now she was stuck about how to combine these.

"It's too much to count," she said.

"How about adding the tens first?" Marilyn said, suggesting a way to help Juanita think about the numbers as tens and ones. "There are forty for the spiders, twenty for the beetles, and twenty for the woodlice. You can do the extra four for the beetles and the eight for the woodlice later." This made sense to Juanita and she combined the tens in her head to get eighty. Then she added the ones to get twenty.

Figure 1–3: Juanita used an approach unique in the class, listing the numbers of all of the creatures' legs in one column.

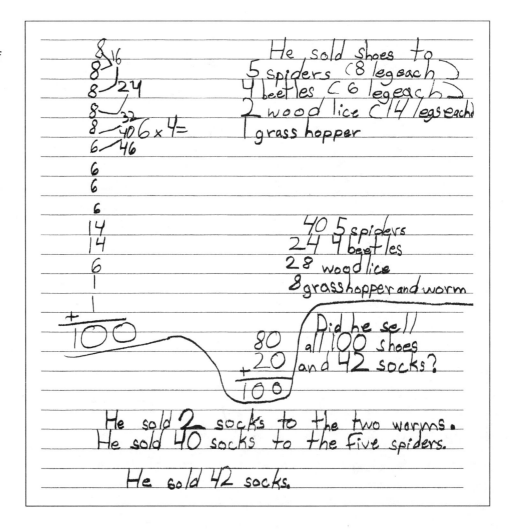

Math and Literature, Grades 2–3

"Do you know how much eighty plus twenty is?" Marilyn asked.

Juanita shook her head "no." "I have to write them down," she said and wrote them one underneath the other and used the standard algorithm to add them. "Look, I got one hundred!" she said with surprise. Watching Juanita was a valuable way for Marilyn to think about how to help her see place value as a tool for making sense of numbers. (See Figure 1–3.)

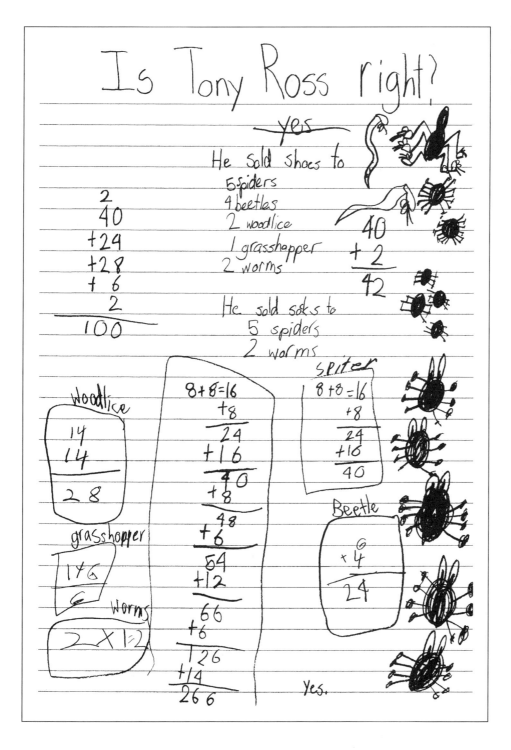

Figure 1–4: On her paper, Julie used a combination of addition and multiplication, and she used detailed drawings as a check.

After a few children had verified that the author had been correct, the rest who were still working then knew that they also should figure out the little centipede sold exactly one hundred shoes and forty-two socks. Knowing the correct answer was an interesting motivation for these children to figure out how to make the numbers work. As children brought their papers to her, Marilyn asked each, "Do you think this problem was easy, hard, or kind of medium?" Their responses were another way for Marilyn to assess their confidence and competence.

Figure 1–4 on page 7 shows how another student approached the problem.

A Cloak for the Dreamer

Taught by Rusty Bresser and Marilyn Burns

A Cloak for the Dreamer, by Aileen Friedman (1994a), is the story of a tailor who has three sons. His older sons, Ivan and Alex, hope to become tailors, but Misha, the youngest, dreams of traveling far and wide. When the Archduke orders new cloaks, the tailor asks his sons for help. Ivan sews a cloak out of rectangular pieces of cloth. Alex uses squares and triangles. Misha fashions his cloak out of circles, and its open spaces make it useless. The tailor finds a geometric way to fix the cloak and allows Misha to fulfill his dream of going out into the world. Rusty Bresser read the story to a class of third graders, presenting them with a context for thinking about geometric shapes and how they fit together. Marilyn Burns shared the book with another third-grade class and led students in a similar investigation.

MATERIALS

A Cloak for the Dreamer Shapes, duplicated on tagboard, 1 sheet per group (see Blackline Master)

12-by-18-inch white drawing paper, 1 sheet per student

optional: pattern blocks

Rusty Bresser read *A Cloak for the Dreamer* to his third graders near the end of the year. During the year, Rusty had provided opportunities for his students to investigate quilting patterns and tessellations. He wondered how these earlier experiences might affect the way his students thought about solving the problem of the holes in Misha's cloak.

Before Rusty started to read the book, he showed the cover to his class. Because the story is about a tailor and his three sons, Rusty asked, "Who can explain what a tailor is?"

Artrina said, "Someone who sews clothes." Others nodded.

Rusty read the story up to the page where Misha has made his cloak of circles. When Rusty showed the class the picture, he asked, "What do you think about Misha's cloak?"

Scott said, "The cloak has holes in it. The Archduke will get water on him."

"He'll get muddy," Amber added.

"It won't work, it's not solid," Mark said.

"I agree that Misha has a problem," Rusty responded. "What do you think he should do about his problem? Who has an idea?"

Makito raised his hand. "I think if he put a blanket on the back of it, it would cover up the holes," he said.

Anna had another idea. She said, "If Misha made more circles, he could sew them on the back where the holes are."

Josh suggested, "He could just make another cloak with rectangles instead of circles."

Mark offered a different solution. "He needs to cut the sides off the circles so they're hexagons," he said. "Then he can sew them together again."

Rusty reported that he thought it was important to give his students the opportunity to verbalize their ideas before asking them to write. "I wanted to have many ideas available," he said. "I think talking about various solutions provides some students with access to an idea that they might not have on their own. It also gives those children who have ideas a chance to formulate them verbally. Verbalization is a helpful support to the writing process."

Rather than continuing to read the story, Rusty asked the children to write letters to Misha offering him a solution to the problem. "When you write to Misha," he told the children, "first explain the problem with the cloak. Then offer Misha a solution and include an illustration to show him what you mean." Rusty asked for questions, and then the class got to work.

As they worked, the children talked to one another, sharing their solutions, talking about the book, and discussing their pictures. Rusty circulated, and as students finished, he had them read their letters aloud to him.

Mark wrote about his idea for turning the circles into hexagons. (See Figure 2–1.)

Jo Ann wrote: *Dear Misha, I have another answer if you lamanate it it could probaly be a rain cloak of the world. from your friind, Jo Ann.*

Sam wrote: *Dear Misha, The problem is you made a holes in the cloak. You should over lap where the holes were.*

"How would that solve his problem?" Rusty asked.

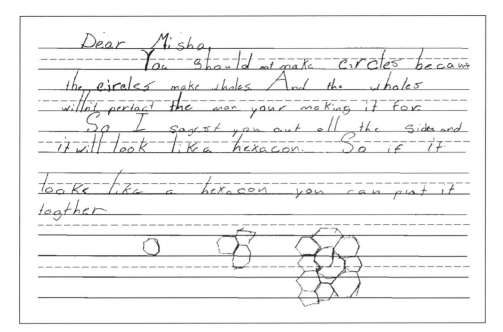

Figure 2–1: Mark suggested that Misha fix the cloak by cutting the sides off the circles to make hexagons.

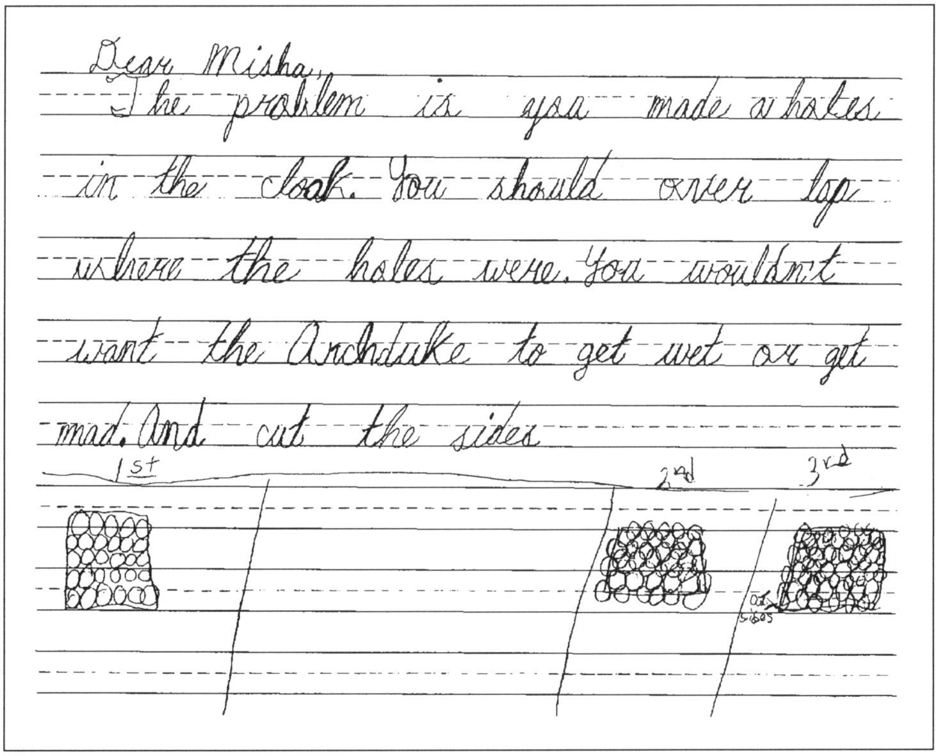

Dear Misha,
You should not make circles becaus the circles make wholes. And the wholes willn't perfact the man your making it for So I sagest you cut all the sides and it will look lika hexacon. So if it

looks lika hexacon you can put it togther

Figure 2–2: Sam suggested that Misha overlap the circles.

Dear Misha,
The problem is you made wholes in the cloak. You should over lap where the holes were. You wouldn't want the Archduke to get wet or get mad. And cut the sides

1st   2nd   3rd

Sam thought for a moment and then decided to write some more about his solution. He added: *You wouldn't want the Archduke to get wet or get mad. And cut the sides.* He drew pictures to show his solution in three steps. (See Figure 2–2.)

Alicia wrote about adding other materials to the cloak. (See Figure 2–3.)

> Dear Misha,
>
> Your cloak has holes in it. What were you thinking! lisen here
>
> bud all you have to do is put plstic that will fit it and then put
>
> a strap and a butin that's all you have to bo o.K.
>
> plastic's allready on it. →
>
> I sugestied plastic because it would not spole the colors and it would not get on it

The Next Day

The next day Rusty called the students together on the rug to share their letters. They were interested in all the different solutions and laughed at several funny ones.

After the children had shared their work, Rusty read the book all the way through, starting over again from the beginning. Mark was excited to see that the tailor solved Misha's problem the same way he had suggested. Rusty let him enjoy this happy discovery but was careful to talk to the class about this not being the only possible answer.

Rusty also asked the children how they felt about stopping in the middle of the book to solve a problem. This is something Rusty does not normally do because he feels it interrupts the flow of the story. The students decided that stopping in the middle was a good idea in this instance.

"It made us curious," Annette said.

"It gave us a reason to listen," Josh added.

Then Rusty presented a second activity. He handed out sheets of 12-by-18-inch white drawing paper and gave each group a piece of tagboard with two sizes of triangles, rectangles, and squares printed on it. (See Blackline Master.) He also gave each group construction paper in several colors.

"Each of you will choose one shape and cut it out of the tagboard," Rusty explained. "Then you'll use the tagboard shape as a pattern to trace and cut more pieces from two different colors of construction paper. Use those shapes to make a pattern of your own for a cloak."

The children enjoyed the activity. They chose their colors carefully, thinking about how they would look together. When they finished making their cloak patterns, they taped them to the wall. The students stood together in small groups, talking about the patterns they especially liked.

"This is kind of like the quilts we made," Danny said.

"In what way?" Rusty asked.

"All of these shapes fit together because the sides are straight," Danny explained.

Reflecting on the experience, Rusty reported, "This task was fairly simple for the students because they had explored quilting patterns earlier in the year. If I do this activity again with children who have had this prior experience, I'll ask them to choose two different shapes for their own patterns. But I know the students enjoyed the activity, and I think it was a good way to see what they remembered from earlier in the year."

Another Lesson with Third Graders

When Marilyn Burns read *A Cloak for the Dreamer* to her class of third graders, she didn't stop as Rusty had, but instead read the story straight through.

Dominic commented at the end of the story, "It's kind of happy and sad at the same time."

"Yeah," Ian added, "the father was happy that his son was going to do what he wanted but sad because he would miss him."

"I agree," Lori said, "but I think it's a little more happy than sad because Misha will get to see the world."

After discussing the story and illustrations, Marilyn presented the students with the opportunity to make cloak patterns of their own.

"You won't have to sew," she told them. "Instead, you'll trace shapes, cut them out of colored paper, and paste them down to make a pattern." She had duplicated onto tagboard the same shapes that Rusty had used. (See Blackline Master.) Also, she told the children they could trace around pattern blocks if they preferred.

Although these third graders had explored shapes and their properties during a geometry unit earlier in the year, they hadn't had any classroom experience with quilt patterns or tessellations. Marilyn chose to use the book to offer the children the chance to investigate piecing shapes together, and she didn't limit the students to using just one shape.

"Try different shapes and see how they can fit together," she told the class. "Then choose the shapes you'll use for your pattern. Remember, the shapes you choose must fit together snugly, with no holes and no overlaps."

Marilyn noticed that the task was easier for some children than for others, both because of the variation in children's spatial experiences and their cutting and pasting skills. She listened as the children talked among themselves about what they noticed.

Annette said to Alberto, "Look, you can line squares up to make long skinny rectangles." She used squares and several sizes of rectangles for her pattern. (See Figure 2–4.) Alberto followed her lead and also used squares and rectangles for his pattern.

Loren showed Lynn her work. "Two triangles make a parallelogram," she commented. "It's a neat shape."

A bit later, Marilyn noticed that Erin was having difficulty pasting her shapes where she wanted to. Erin said to Stewart, "You have to put them perfect or it comes out wrong. This can be very frustrating." Stewart nodded sympathetically and returned to working on his pattern. Erin kept working on hers as well.

Jack was also having difficulty managing the shapes. Unlike Erin, however, he didn't keep at it, but instead spent his time snipping the

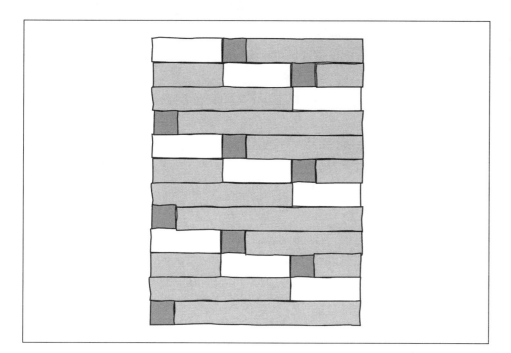

shapes into random sizes. His desk was covered with bits of colored paper. Marilyn knelt by his side.

"It's too hard," Jack said. "I can't get them to go right."

"There's a kind of design you can make using all those bits and pieces," Marilyn said. "It's not a repeating pattern, but it has a name. It's called a crazy quilt. Why don't you try to see if you can fit together the pieces you cut?"

This seemed to relieve Jack's frustration for the moment, and he got back to work. He didn't finish, however. The task seemed too difficult for him, and Marilyn chose not to push him.

"He just wasn't interested enough to stick with it," Marilyn reported, "and I didn't want to risk having the experience kill his interest in exploring shapes. Jack needs more experience with concrete materials before being asked to complete a project like this."

After the children finished their patterns, Marilyn had them write about what they had discovered.

Annie had pieced together hexagons and two sizes of triangles. She wrote: *When I put the shaps together I saw a Cristmas tree, a Ice creme cone and a Big Big triangle.* (See Figure 2–5.)

Javier wrote: *I discovered that some shapes don't fit together.*

Seiji was more specific. He wrote: *I discovered that squares don't fit on hexegons but diamonds fit on hexegons. I discovered that 6 diamonds, 6 hexegons and 6 triangles will make a big hexegon. And I discovered 6 triangles will make a hexegon.*

Jack wrote: *Well, mine turned out not to work. It was kind of weird. Everytime I had a great idea, it never worked and the more I tried to patch it up, it made it worse.*

Figure 2–5: Annie saw Christmas trees and ice cream cones in her pattern.

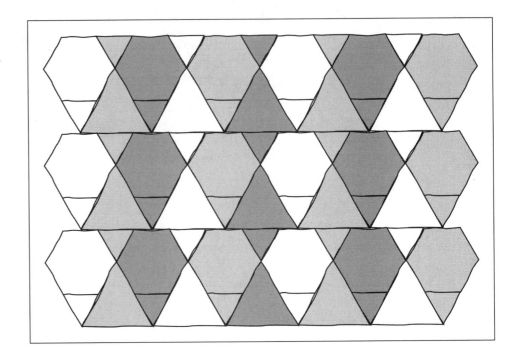

Figure 2–6: Daniel sketched his pattern and wrote about his discoveries.

A Cloak for the Dreamer

① A couple of the shapes I used ② were traingles, diamonds and hexagons this is the way I fitt them together

③ I had to plan it all before I did it becaase if I hadn't It probably wouldn't of fit together. A couple of the discoveries I made were......... for one thing you cant cumbind a saqare with a hexagon. You cant even cubind a saqare with a diamond a traingle or veriouse other shaper.

Daniel made a sketch of his pattern and wrote: *I had to plan it all before I did it because if I hadn't It probably wouldn't of fit together. A couple of the discoveries I made were . . . for one thing you cant cumbind a square with a hexagon. You cant even cubind a square with a diamond a traingle or <u>veriouse</u> other shapes.* (See Figure 2–6.)

(**Note:** *A Cloak for the Dreamer* provides the basis for two whole-class lessons and an independent menu activity in *Math by All Means: Geometry, Grades 1–2*, by Chris Confer [1994]. See the References for additional information.)

The 512 Ants on Sullivan Street

Taught by Marilyn Burns

Carol Losi's book *The 512 Ants on Sullivan Street* (1997) describes, in rollicking rhyme, how ants pilfer the contents of a picnic basket as it is being carried to a picnic on Sullivan Street. First 1 ant carries off a crumb, then 2 ants take pieces of plum, and the rhyme continues along with the number pattern, with the number of ants doubling to 4, 8, 16, and so on, until 512 ants carry off an entire fudge cake. Marilyn Burns read the story to a class of third graders and engaged them in an activity for exploring doubles.

MATERIALS

*T*he 512 Ants on Sullivan Street is a rhyming story with repeating refrains. For example, after introducing the capers of one ant and then two ants, the rhyme continues:

> *There go 4 ants with a barbecued chip,*
> *They held it above them so they wouldn't trip.*
> *They trailed the 2 ants with some pieces of plum,*
> *who followed 1 ant who carried a crumb. . . .*

Marilyn invited the class of third graders to join in as the story progressed, and soon most of them were chanting the repeating rhymes. Also, some began predicting the next number of ants, with some students guessing randomly and others figuring, some correctly and some incorrectly. For example, after the verse above, Julie said, "I bet there will be eight next."

"Nope, I think it will be twenty-four," Zack said.

"I think thirty-two," Travon said.

Marilyn didn't comment about the pattern at this time but continued with the story to give more of the students a chance to think about what was happening numerically. The children enjoyed the story, especially at the end, when there was nothing for the people to munch while the ants were having a feast in their ant hole.

After finishing the book, Marilyn revisited the story, recording on the board so that the students could analyze the numerical pattern. For each number of ants up to sixteen, she recorded each on the board and showed how the next number came from doubling the previous number of ants. When she wrote *16 + 16*, she left the answer for the students to figure.

$$1$$
$$1 + 1 = 2$$
$$2 + 2 = 4$$
$$4 + 4 = 8$$
$$8 + 8 = 16$$
$$16 + 16 =$$

"How much is sixteen plus sixteen?" Marilyn asked. After about a third of the students had raised their hands, she said, "Talk with the others at your table about the answer." She gave the students time to talk and then asked them to say the answer together in a whisper voice. Then she asked for volunteers to explain how they figured out the sum. She continued in this way for the next several numbers. As children explained their reasoning, Marilyn recorded their ideas on the board.

For example, for the problem of adding 128 + 128, four children presented their ideas. Julie explained that she would write the numbers one underneath the other. Marilyn did this on the board, and Julie then explained how she would use the standard algorithm to find the sum.

Antonio explained that he would use a friendlier number. "I'd use one hundred thirty," he said. Antonio easily added 130 and 130 in his head to get 260, then got confused for a moment, but finally figured out that he needed to subtract 4 from 260 to get 256.

Travon had a different way of figuring. "I added one hundred plus one hundred, and that's two hundred," he began. "Then I added twenty-eight to twenty-eight, and I know that's fifty-six. So then it's easy. The answer is two hundred fifty-six."

Danielle explained that her way was like Travon's. "Except I added the two twenties by themselves and then the two sixes," she said.

After the children had explained how they figured 256 + 256, Marilyn asked, "What if we continued the pattern? What would we have to add next?" The children knew that next they would add 512 + 512 and, conferring in pairs, they were able to figure out the answer. Marilyn added the problem to the list.

$$1$$
$$1 + 1 = 2$$
$$2 + 2 = 4$$
$$4 + 4 = 8$$
$$8 + 8 = 16$$
$$16 + 16 = 32$$
$$32 + 32 = 64$$
$$64 + 64 = 128$$
$$128 + 128 = 256$$
$$256 + 256 = 512$$
$$512 + 512 = 1,024$$

Marilyn then asked the children to compare the sums for these problems to two other friendly numbers—100 and 1,000. She began by asking, "Which of the sums is closest to one hundred?" The children agreed that 128 was closest to 100 and that 128 was 28 more than 100. But when Marilyn asked how they knew that 128 was closer to 100 than 64, most weren't able to explain why. This indicated to Marilyn that the children needed further work with subtraction, which is always more difficult for children than addition or even multiplication.

"Which sum on our list is closest to one thousand?" Marilyn asked. The children agreed that it was 1,024, and it seemed clear to them that 512 was much farther away. "It's hundreds away," Juanita offered. On the list, Marilyn circled the sum of 128 and wrote *100* next to it and then circled 1,024 and wrote *1,000* next it. She did this to model for the children what they would need to do on their individual assignment.

$$1 + 1 = 2$$
$$2 + 2 = 4$$
$$4 + 4 = 8$$
$$8 + 8 = 16$$
$$16 + 16 = 32$$
$$32 + 32 = 64$$
$$64 + 64 = \boxed{128} \qquad 100$$
$$128 + 128 = 256$$
$$256 + 256 = 512$$
$$512 + 512 = \boxed{1,024} \qquad 1,000$$

Marilyn then presented the assignment. "Now you'll explore your own numerical doubling pattern," she said and wrote on the board:

2   3   4   5   6   7   8   9   10

She said, "First I thought that all of these would be good starting numbers, but then I realized that if you chose two, four, or eight, you'd be doubling the same numbers as in the pattern from the book." She crossed out the 2, 4, and 8. "You can choose any of the other numbers for your starting number," Marilyn continued, leaving 6 as a choice even though it would produce the same pattern as starting with 3. Marilyn also marked the numbers for their difficulty and explained, "The two-star numbers are the most difficult, the one-star numbers are of medium difficulty, and the numbers without stars are the easiest."

~~2~~   3*   ~~4~~   5   6*   7**   ~~8~~   9**   10

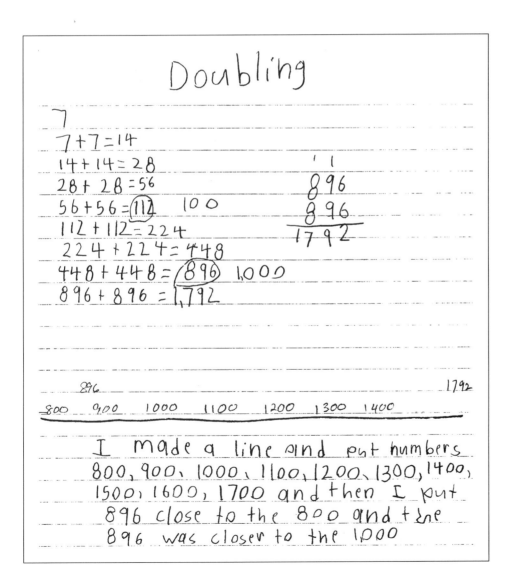

Figure 3–1: Isaac chose 7, one of the harder numbers. He made a number line to show why 896 was closer to 1,000 than 1,792.

Marilyn continued with the directions. "After you pick your number, double it, and then double the sum, and continue until you get a sum that is greater than one thousand. Then circle the numbers that are closest to one hundred and one thousand, as I did. Finally, if you can, explain how far each of the numbers you circled is away from either one hundred or one thousand."

The students got to work. They were able to do the addition pattern for their numbers, but it was difficult for many of them to explain how far their circled numbers were from one hundred or one thousand. Figures 3–1 through 3–4 show how several students tackled this problem.

Figure 3–2: Daria's number pattern was correct, but her explanations showed her confusion with figuring how far away 56 is from 100 and how far away 896 is from 1,000.

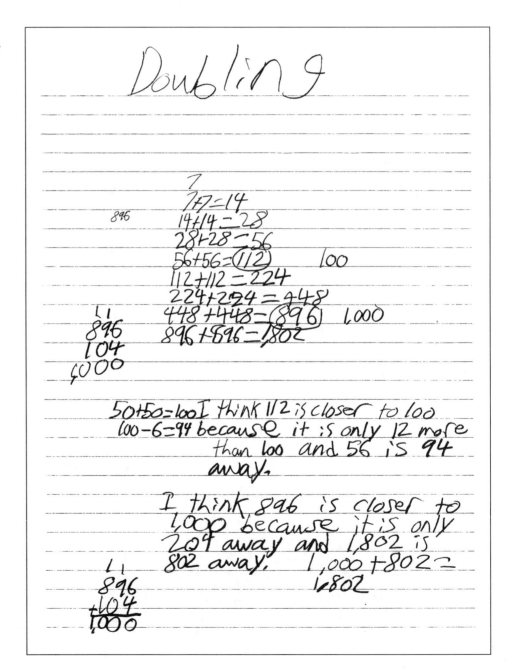

Math and Literature, Grades 2–3

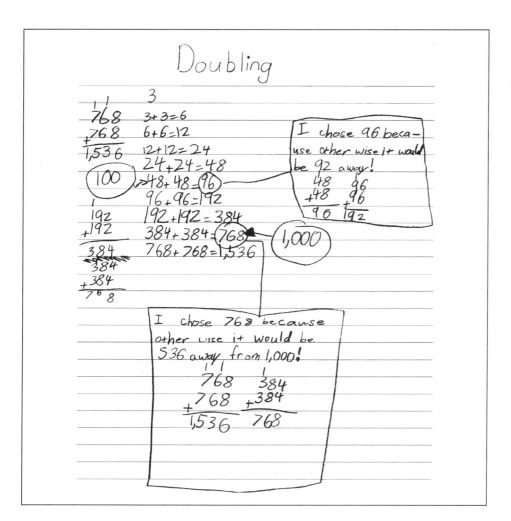

Figure 3–3: Priscilla chose the number three and completed the assignment correctly.

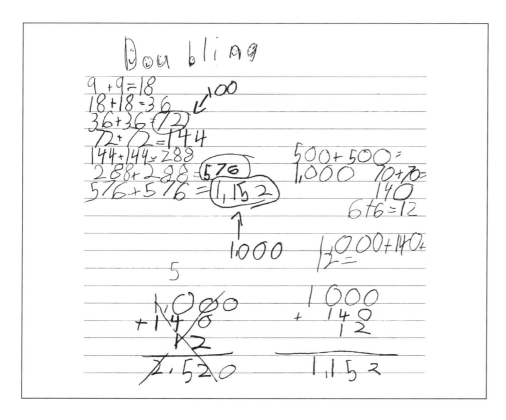

Figure 3–4: Ana's paper showed the error she made figuring out 576 + 576. She broke the numbers apart, adding 500 + 500, 70 + 70, and 6 + 6, but then she lined up the partial sums incorrectly to get 2,520. Travon helped her do the addition correctly.

The Greedy Triangle

Taught by Stephanie Sheffield

The Greedy Triangle, by Marilyn Burns (1994), is a story about a triangle who always wishes for more. At the beginning of the story, the triangle supports bridges, makes music in symphony orchestras, catches the wind for sailboats, and much, much more. After a while, however, the triangle becomes dissatisfied and is sure that if it had one more side and one more angle, its life would be far more interesting. The local shapeshifter grants the triangle's wish and turns it into a quadrilateral, then a pentagon, then a hexagon, and so on, until the shape finally learns that being a triangle is best after all. Stephanie Sheffield read the book to a class of second graders and then engaged the students in exploring shapes.

MATERIALS

triangles cut from construction paper in various shapes, colors, and sizes, with no side longer than 3 inches, 2–3 per student

Stephanie gathered the second graders on the rug to read *The Greedy Triangle* to them. The first spread of the book introduces the triangle and describes some of the places that triangles occur in the world—roofs, bridges, symphony orchestras, sailboats, slices of pie, and halves of sandwiches. The students looked carefully at the illustration for examples of each of the triangle's roles.

"Look," Ramon said. "There are triangles in those derricks, too." He was pleased to spot something in the illustration that hadn't been mentioned in the story.

The children listened attentively as Stephanie continued reading. The next page tells the triangle's favorite thing to do—slipping into place when people put their hands on their hips. Stephanie asked

Becky to stand up and put her hands on her hips. Then she traced the triangle formed by Becky's body and each section of her bent arms.

"Can you see the triangle?" Stephanie asked. Most of the children nodded and a few put their own hands on their hips to test the idea.

Stephanie refocused the students on the illustration and asked, "Where else do you see triangles?" The students pointed out triangles as roofs, as a mountaintop, as trees, and on the prince's crown.

After reading the page where the triangle wishes for one more angle and one more side, Stephanie paused. "What would the triangle look like if its wish were granted?" she asked the students.

"A square!" several students answered.

"Could it be any other shape?" she asked. "Raise your hand if you have an idea." The children were familiar with rectangles and also with the names of the pattern block shapes, and Stephanie was curious if they would relate any of this information to her questions. They were quiet for a moment, and then some hands began to go up. Stephanie called on Anna.

"It could be a rectangle," she said.

"Oh yeah," several children commented.

"That was my idea," Will said, putting his hand down. Now no one had a hand raised.

"Think about our pattern block shapes," Stephanie prompted. "Do any of them have four sides?" Hands shot up.

"It could be a blue diamond," Raul said.

"Do you know another name for the blue diamond?" Stephanie asked.

"Parallelogram," Raul said, carefully pronouncing the word.

Martha got excited. "I know," she said, "it could be a trapezoid."

"Let's see what the book says," Stephanie said and read, "Poof! The shapeshifter turned the triangle into a quadrilateral." Stephanie wrote *quadrilateral* on the board, said it aloud, and asked the children to pronounce it. She also wrote a *4* and explained, "All of the shapes you mentioned—square, rectangle, parallelogram, and trapezoid—have four sides. Four-sided shapes like these are all called quadrilaterals." Stephanie then gave the children time to examine the illustration for examples of quadrilaterals.

Stephanie continued in this way, asking children to predict the new shape each time the triangle asked the shapeshifter to give him another side, then recording the name of the shape on the board and giving the children time to examine the illustration carefully. She listed the names of all of the shapes that occurred in the story.

The children giggled when the shape had too many sides to keep its balance and began to roll down the hill. When the shape finally returned to being a triangle, a few of the children clapped. Stephanie added *triangle* to the list. Then she said, "Here's another new word. All of these shapes are also called *polygons*. Even though they have different numbers of sides, they all have straight sides. And they all enclose a space, the way a fence does." Stephanie wrote *Polygon* to title the list.

Polygon
triangle	*3*
quadrilateral	*4*
pentagon	*5*
hexagon	*6*
heptagon	*7*
octagon	*8*
nonagon	*9*
decagon	*10*

Stephanie then talked with the children about the prefixes—*tri-, quad-, penta-, hexa-, octa-,* and so on. "What other words do you know that begin with these prefixes?" she asked. The children brainstormed words and Stephanie talked with them about what they meant.

Stephanie then showed the children the triangles that she had cut out of construction paper. She had cut out lots of triangles in different shapes and sizes so that the children would have an ample supply from which to choose. She spread them out in a box lid for the children to see.

Stephanie explained to the students what they were to do. "There are enough triangles so that everyone can choose one," she told them. "You'll each choose one of these triangles, take it to your desk, and then turn it around to look at it from different angles." Stephanie took a triangle from the supply and modeled doing this for the children.

She continued, "Think about what your triangle might be a part of. When you have an idea, get a piece of white paper from the art supplies. Then go back to your desk, glue the triangle down, and draw a picture around it to show where your triangle is. Then write a sentence to describe your picture."

The children were eager to get started. Stephanie dismissed them from the rug one by one, having each child choose a triangle before returning to his or her seat. Some children, like Hassan, began drawing right away, sure of the pictures in their minds. Other children, however, took several minutes to look at their triangles, turning them over and thinking about what to do with them. Some watched their friends and borrowed ideas from others at their tables.

The results were varied and delightful. Scott pictured his triangle as part of the pleated skirt of a cheerleader. (See Figure 4–1.) Reed drew

Figure 4–1: Scott wrote:
*This is his favorit thing to
do stick on a cheerleader
skirt.*

Figure 4–2: Reed wrote:
*My pictur is a penguin the
triangle is the beak.*

his as the beak of a penguin. (See Figure 4–2.) Antonio's triangle
became an escalator in a department store. Janine drew a playground
scene. (See Figure 4–3.)

It's important for children to understand that geometry is a part of
the world around them, and this book helped children make this

Figure 4–3: Janine wrote: *This is a slide that children can play on in the summer time.*

connection. Also, integrating art and mathematics was effective for helping the children develop their spatial reasoning.

(**Note:** In *Math by All Means: Geometry, Grades 3–4,* by Cheryl Rectanus [1994], *The Greedy Triangle* provides the basis for a whole-class lesson in which students rewrite and illustrate the story. See the References for more information.)

How Big Is a Foot?

Taught by Bonnie Tank and Lynne Zolli

In the book *How Big Is a Foot?* Rolf Myller (1962) tells the story of a king who wants to give his queen a very special birthday present. This amusing and ingenious story presents a dilemma that engages children in thinking about measurement, ratio, and proportion. Bonnie Tank read the book to a second-grade class and Lynne Zolli introduced it to her third graders. Then both classes worked on a problem-solving activity involving measurement.

MATERIALS

none

In *How Big Is a Foot,* the King faces a problem as the Queen's birthday approaches: What can he give to someone who has everything? He is pleased when he thinks of having a bed made for her. At the time of the story, beds hadn't yet been invented, so the Queen certainly didn't have one already.

To figure how big the bed should be, the King asks the Queen to put on her new pajamas and lie down on the floor. Using his paces, he measures and finds that the bed must be six of his feet long and three of his feet wide to be big enough to fit the Queen (including her crown, which the Queen sometimes likes to wear to bed).

The apprentice who makes the bed, however, is a good deal smaller than the King. He carefully measures six of his feet for the length and three of his feet for the width and builds a beautiful bed, but it is too small. The King is so angry that he has the apprentice thrown into jail.

Sitting in the jail cell, the apprentice thinks and thinks and finally realizes what the problem is. He comes up with a solution and makes a new bed. It is the right size for the Queen and is ready just in time for her birthday. The King is so pleased that he releases the apprentice from jail and makes him a royal prince.

Bonnie didn't read the entire story to the second-grade class but stopped once the apprentice went to jail. She talked with the children about the apprentice's problem and had them offer their suggestions. Bonnie then asked that they each write a letter to the apprentice and offer him advice. Their letters revealed different approaches to the problem.

Leslie explained what the apprentice should have done. She wrote: *Why was the bed so small? The king was very mad. Apprentice feet were very small! You should have measure with a ruler.*

Brandon put the responsibility on the King. He wrote: *I no why your in jail. Because your foot is to small. The bed is to small. The king should have measured with your foot.*

In his letter, Dominic also included advice about what the King should do. He wrote: *I think I know how to get you out of jail. Your feet are smaller than the king's feet. So tell the king that you messed up on the bed. And please could I have another chance at the bed. And ask him when you make it he has to measure the wood so it will be the right size.* (See Figure 5–1.)

Max gave the apprentice specific advice about how to address the King. He wrote: *The bed whes [was] too small because yor feet are to small and the kings feet are bigger then yhour feet. Soew the idea is you ask the jaler to let you tik [talk] to the king and you can tell the king avry thing I told you. just sae I have too yose yor feet.*

Jennifer gave a mathematical solution that maintained the correct proportion between the length and the width. She wrote: *I am sorry that you are in jail, I think you sould make a new bed. The bed sould be ten feet long and five feet wide.*

Figure 5–1: In his letter, Dominic gave the apprentice advice for negotiating with the king.

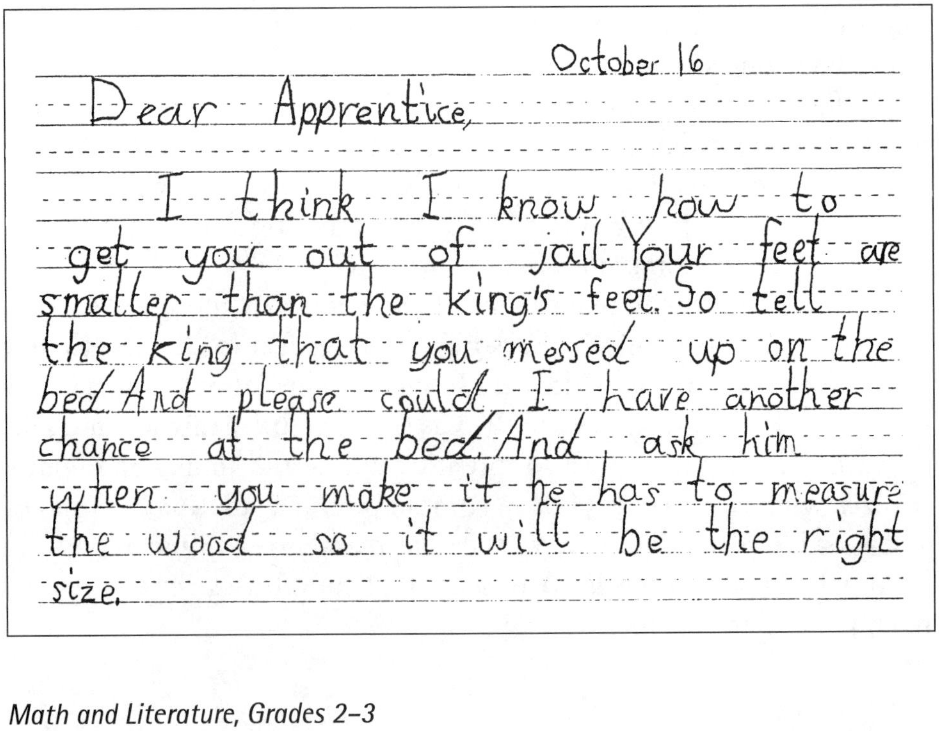

October 16

Dear Apprentice,

I think I know how to get you out of jail. Your feet are smaller than the king's feet. So tell the king that you messed up on the bed. And please could I have another chance at the bed. And ask him when you make it he has to measure the wood so it will be the right size.

After the children completed the assignment, Bonnie read the rest of the story to the class.

The Lesson with Third Graders

Lynne conducted the same activity with her class of third graders. Her students included some different suggestions in their letters. Bolan, for example, wrote: *The bed was to small because your feet were to small for the queen. You can ask the king for one more chance. But this time ask the king to use his feet.* Bolan included a sketch to illustrate the comparison between six of the king's feet and six of the apprentice's feet. He also included a postscript: *P.S. if this dasen't work have a nice time in the bighouse.* (See Figure 5–2.)

In his letter, Jon gave advice and revealed his interest in Roman numerals. He wrote: *Show your king the difference in size. Now have your king step in paint and make a rectangle VI feet long and III feet wide. Now build the bed that size.*

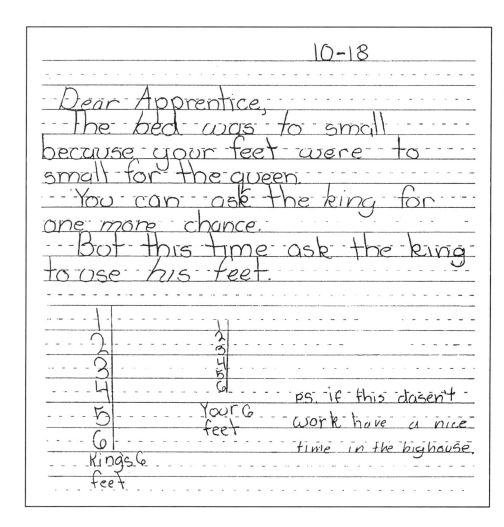

Figure 5–2: Bolan included a sketch to show the difference between six of the king's feet and six of the apprentice's feet.

Figure 5–3: Matthew was
one of the children who
suggested using a ruler.

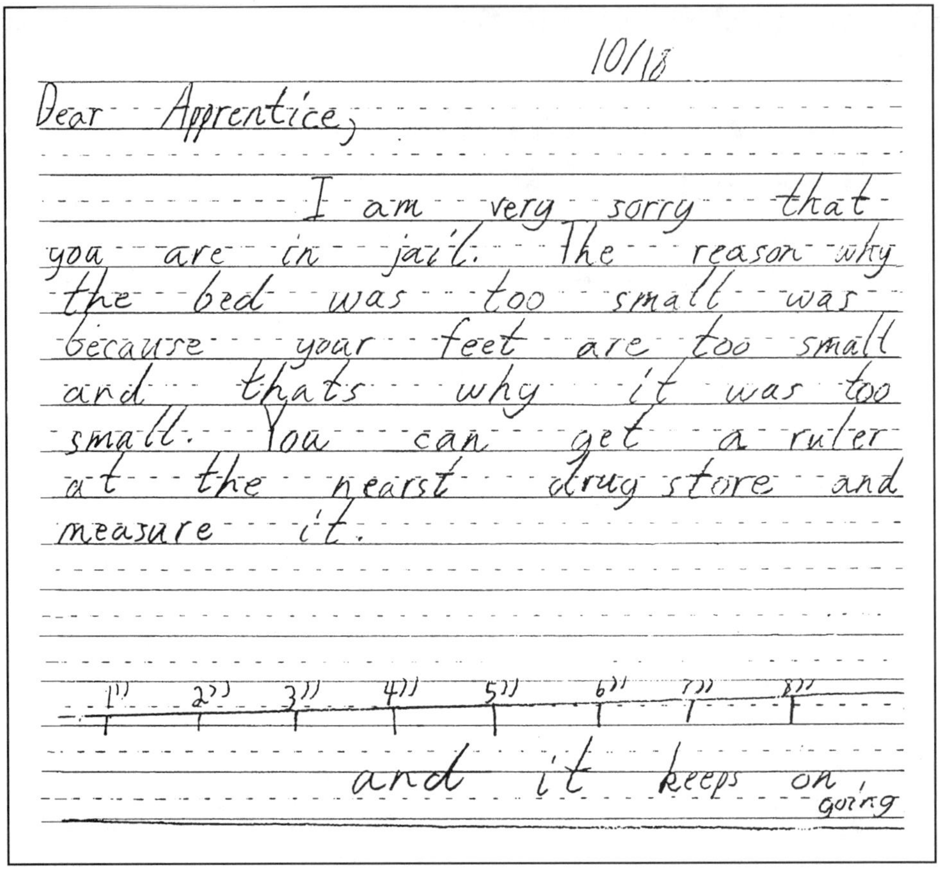

10/18

Dear Apprentice,

          I am very sorry that
you are in jail. The reason why
the bed was too small was
because your feet are too small
and thats why it was too
small. You can get a ruler
at the nearst drug store and
measure it.

1"   2"   3"   4"   5"   6"   7"   8"

and it keeps on, going

Several of the children suggested the apprentice use a ruler.
Matthew, for example, wrote: *I am very sorry that you are in jail. The
reason why the bed was too small was because your feet are too small
and thats why it was too small. You can get a ruler at the nearst drug-
store and measure it.* He drew a picture of a ruler. (See Figure 5–3.)

Eric wrote: *I think I can help you get out of jail if you invent a ruler.
You ask for some wood that is 12 inch tall. And that will be a ruler.*

Instead of offering advice, Wanda explained the problem and con-
centrated her effort on her illustration. She wrote: *Your foot is to small
to do like the king. And the kings foot is to big and your foot is to
small to do it. That is your prublems.* (See Figure 5–4.)

After the children completed the assignment, Lynne read the rest of
the story to the class and discussed with them the solution in the book.
She also used the book to talk with the students about the benefits of
using standard units to measure and to communicate about measurements. She asked them to estimate the length of their own beds and
then had them find out for homework.

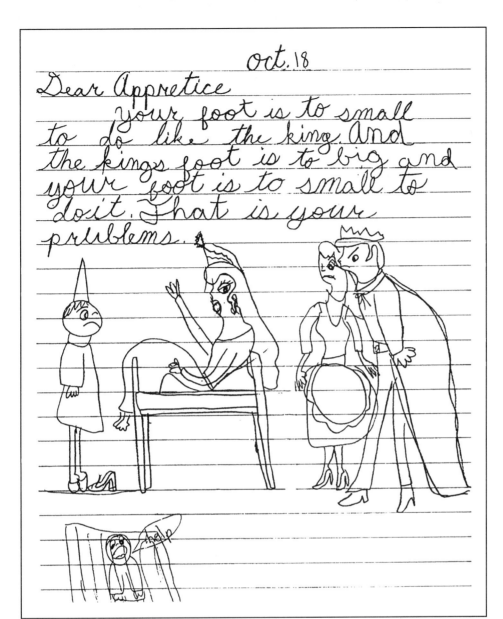

Oct. 18

Dear Appretice
  Your foot is to small
to do like the king. And
the kings foot is to big and
your foot is to small to
do it. That is your
priblems.

Figure 5–4: Wanda's letter focused on describing the problem, both in words and with an illustration.

Inch by Inch
Taught by Marilyn Burns

Illustrated with vibrant cutouts on white backgrounds, Leo Lionni's *Inch by Inch* (1994) tells the story of an inchworm who is able to measure anything and proves it by measuring a robin's tail, a flamingo's neck, a toucan's beak, a heron's legs, a pheasant's tail, and the entire length of a hummingbird. When confronted with the challenge of either measuring a nightingale's song or being eaten, the inchworm creatively solves his problem. Marilyn Burns read the book to a class of third graders and used it to engage the students in estimating and measuring lengths in inches.

MATERIALS

12-inch rulers, 1 per student
1-inch color tiles, 1 per student

When Marilyn showed the cover of *Inch by Inch* to the class of third graders, Ana said, "I see the inchworm. He's up there on the grass."

"Me, too," several others added.

"I know about that medal," Zack said, referring to the Caldecott medal on the book's cover. "It has a person riding on a horse and it's a special award."

"The librarian told us about the prize," Hallie added.

Marilyn said, "It's called a Caldecott award and it was given to the artist for his wonderful illustrations in this book."

Marilyn then read the story to the class. She opened the book to the first spread and read about the hungry robin who was about to eat the inchworm. "Do you see the inchworm?" she asked the children, pointing to the inchworm sitting on a twig. The children nodded.

"It's on the branch," Travon commented.

"The robin is trying to eat him," William added.

Marilyn turned to the next page, which reveals that the inchworm talks his way out of being eaten by convincing the robin that he is useful. "I measure things," the inchworm says. The robin demands that the inchworm measure his tail, and the following spread shows him doing so, inching down the tail and counting, "One, two, three, four, five inches."

The robin is so pleased that, with the inchworm on his back, he flies to where other birds need to be measured. The next five spreads show the inchworm measuring the neck of a flamingo, the beak of a toucan, the legs of a heron, the tail of a pheasant, and the length of a hummingbird.

But when the inchworm meets the nightingale, the nightingale presents him with an unusual challenge: "Measure my song or I'll eat you for breakfast." The inchworm is stumped at first. He knows how to measure things, but not songs. Then he has an idea. He asks the nightingale to start singing, and as the nightingale sings, the inchworm measures away through the grass, inch by inch, until he is safely out of sight.

"He got away," Andrea said when Marilyn finished reading.

"He was sneaking away and the nightingale didn't even notice," Antonio said.

"Maybe he was just inching away until the end of the song," Daria said. "Maybe that's how he was measuring—until the song stopped."

"I think he was just escaping," Antonio said.

"Well, at least he's safe," Julie said.

Marilyn then asked the children, "What do you know about what an inch is?"

"There are twelve inches in a foot," Warren said. None of the others had a comment.

Marilyn held up a 1-inch color tile. The children were familiar with the tiles from using them extensively for learning about multiplication. "Our color tiles help me remember how long an inch is," she said. "Each edge of a color tile measures one inch."

Marilyn held the color tile next to her thumb. "Is my thumb an inch long?" she asked.

"No!" the children responded.

"It's longer," Miranda said.

"Yes, my thumb is longer than one inch," Marilyn replied. Then she bent her thumb and held the color tile to show the children that the distance from the tip of her thumb to the knuckle was just about 1 inch. "But this part of my thumb measures just about one inch," she said. "If I ever forget how long an inch is, then I bend my thumb like this, take a look, and then I remember. So I'm carrying an inch around with me all the time." Some of the children were now examining their own bent thumbs.

Next, Marilyn distributed a color tile to each child. "See if the distance from the tip of your thumb to the knuckle is about one inch," she said. The children were delighted to learn that this distance measured just about 1 inch on their own thumbs. As Marilyn went around the room collecting the tiles, she said, "So you don't need these tiles to remind you how long an inch is. You've got an inch with you all the time."

Marilyn then talked with the children about rulers. The class supply of rulers stood in an empty coffee can covered with contact paper. There was a wide assortment. Some measured only inches; some measured only centimeters; some measured inches on one edge and centimeters on the other. Also, some of the inch rulers had marks only for halves and quarters, while others had marks for eighths and sixteenths as well. A few of the rulers began the measurement marks slightly in from the end, which can pose problems for students who are accustomed to lining up the end of the ruler with the end of what they're measuring without paying attention to the lines. Rather than removing the rulers that might pose problems, Marilyn chose to talk with the children about the differences among them. She chose one of the inch rulers with marks just for halves and quarters.

"We can use rulers like this one to measure things and find out how many inches long they are," she said. She held up a pencil.

"Is this pencil longer than one inch?" she asked.

"Yes," the children chorused.

"It looks like it's eight or nine inches," Travon said.

"I think it might be only seven, or maybe five inches," Daria said.

After all the children who wanted to had offered their opinions, Marilyn said, "What you're doing now is estimating how many inches long the pencil is. What do I mean by *estimating*?"

"It's like making a guess," Juanita said.

"You're not really sure but you're trying to be close," Dawn added.

"That's right," Marilyn said. "An estimate is a guess. I think that the pencil is about six inches. But to find out how long the pencil really is, I can use a ruler. First I carefully line up the pencil and the ruler, like this." She held the pencil horizontally and held the ruler beneath it with the end of the ruler lined up with the point on the pencil.

"Then I use the numbers on the ruler to tell me how long the pencil is," she said.

"It's almost seven but not quite," Antonio said.

"It's six and a half," Hiro declared.

"I think it's six and three-quarters," William said.

Marilyn said, "I think it's really close to six and a half." The pencil was actually a little closer to $6\frac{3}{4}$ inches, but William was one of only a few children who had a sense of fractions beyond one-half and Marilyn didn't want to confuse the others. She hoped that the children's experience with measuring would also give them experience with fractions, but at this time she wanted to focus just on measuring and becoming familiar with inches.

"My estimate was off by only one-half of an inch," Marilyn said. She turned to the chalkboard, drew a four-column chart, titled it *Inch by Inch* and labeled the four columns *Thing, Estimate, Actual,* and *How Far Off?*

Inch by Inch

Thing	Estimate	Actual	How Far Off?

"So the first thing that I measured was the pencil," Marilyn said, recording *pencil* in the first column. "And my estimate was six inches," she continued. "I can record that in one of three ways." She wrote next to the chart:

6 inches
6 in.
6"

Marilyn explained, "You can write six inches the first way, spelling out the word for *inches*. Or you can abbreviate *inches* as I did in the second way, or you can abbreviate *inches* by making what looks like a quotation mark as I did in the third way. I think I'll record on the chart the third way." Marilyn wrote *6"* in the second column.

"And what was my actual measurement?" she asked.

"Six and a half," several children chorused.

"Six and a half what?" Marilyn asked.

"Inches," they replied. Marilyn recorded $6\frac{1}{2}$" in the third column.

"How far off was my estimate from my measurement?" she asked.

"One-half inch," several replied. Marilyn recorded $\frac{1}{2}$" in the fourth column.

"I don't worry about my estimate not being exact," Marilyn said. "I try to be close, but I wasn't wrong because my estimate and the actual measurement were different."

Marilyn then modeled estimating, measuring, and recording for another object. "Let me think about the height of the box of tissues," she said, holding up the box for the children to see. Several called out suggestions, and Marilyn said, "I think I'll use three inches for my estimate." Marilyn knew that the box was three inches tall and purposely demonstrated estimating the actual measurement. She drew a line under the information about the pencil and recorded *tissue box* and *3"* in the first two columns.

"Now I'll measure," she said. She held the ruler vertically and the children sitting closest could see that the box was indeed 3 inches tall.

"So my actual measurement is the same as my estimate this time," Marilyn said. She recorded *3"* in the Actual column.

"How far off was I?" she asked.

"You weren't off at all," Travon said.

"You guessed exactly right," Hallie said.

"So that's a bingo," Marilyn said and wrote *Bingo* in the fourth column.

Inch by Inch

Thing	Estimate	Actual	How Far Off?
pencil	6"	$6\frac{1}{2}$"	$\frac{1}{2}$"
tissue box	3"	3"	Bingo

Marilyn then talked with the children about the variety of rulers in the can. She chose a ruler with eighths and sixteenths also indicated and used it to measure the height of the box of tissues. "It's still three inches," Daria said.

Marilyn held up the two rulers side by side so that the children could compare them. She pointed out that the inches were the same on both, but that the second ruler had marks for smaller parts of inches. William and Ana knew about the fractional parts, but none of the others had heard of eighths or sixteenths.

"You don't have to pay attention to all of the marks to do your measurements," Marilyn said. "If you'd rather use a ruler without all of these marks, that's fine, too. But you have to be careful to choose a ruler that measures in inches." She then held up a centimeter ruler.

"See where the one is on this ruler?" she asked.

"It's too close to the edge," Priscilla said.

"It's smaller," Andrea added.

"This ruler doesn't measure in inches," Marilyn said. "It measures in centimeters. We'll learn about them another day. Be sure when you take a ruler that you take one that measures in inches. To check, use your thumb and be sure that the distance from the tip of your thumb to the knuckle lands on the one on the ruler."

Marilyn then took a ruler from the can with the starting mark a bit inside the edge. She pointed out to the children that they had to line up this starting mark with one edge of what they were measuring, and she modeled doing this with the tissue box. "Take care when you use one of these rulers," she said.

Then Marilyn drew another row on the chart so she could record another measurement. "Now I'm going to try to estimate the length of something that's far away," she said. "This is harder, and you may want to give yourself this kind of challenge, too." Marilyn looked around the room and decided on the fan tacked to the bulletin board next to the poster of Kyoto. She said, "I'm going to estimate that the height of the fan, from the bottom of the handle to the top of the fan, is about twelve inches."

On the chart, Marilyn recorded *fan* and *12"*. Then she walked over to the bulletin board and held up the ruler. Clearly, the fan was longer than 12 inches. Marilyn modeled how to measure. She placed the ruler so one end was at the top of the fan and held it with one hand while, with a finger of her other hand, she marked where the ruler ended. Then she moved the ruler to measure the rest. There were 3 extra inches.

"That's fifteen," Ana said.

"You were off by three," Mattie said.

Marilyn repeated what the girls said, emphasizing the word *inches* each time. "Yes, the fan is fifteen *inches* tall and I was off by three *inches*." She returned to the chart, recorded these measurements, and drew two more lines to indicate where she could record the data for two more items.

Inch by Inch

Thing	Estimate	Actual	How Far Off?
pencil	6"	$6\frac{1}{2}$"	$\frac{1}{2}$"
tissue box	3"	3"	Bingo
fan	12"	15"	3"

Then she said to the children, "You're each to make a chart of your own. Then you'll choose things to estimate, measure, and figure out how far off you are, and record on your chart. If you want a challenge, choose longer things, but don't choose anything longer than one of the supply drawers."

"Can we measure a book?" Warren wanted to know.

"That would be fine," Marilyn answered.

"How many things do we measure?" Julie asked.

"At least five," Marilyn said, "but you can do more if you'd like."

"Can we draw a picture on the chart of what we measure?" Zack asked, always interested in drawing.

"Yes," Marilyn responded.

There were no more questions. Before having the children get to work, Marilyn did a quick assessment. "Hold your fingers up so that they are just about one inch apart," she said. She scanned the room to check that all of the children did this correctly.

She then said, "Now hold your fingers so that they are about three inches apart." Again she scanned the room.

"And now show twelve inches, which is one foot, the length of the ruler," she said. Satisfied that the children could closely estimate 1 inch, 3 inches, and 12 inches, Marilyn asked Daria to distribute unlined paper to everyone while she went around the room with the can of rulers, allowing each child to choose one to use.

The children got busy making their charts. This was difficult for some of the children, but Marilyn felt that it was better to have them struggle with making their own charts than to give them a prepared worksheet. It's beneficial for children to learn to organize their own papers.

Fractional measurements posed problems for some of the students. When Marilyn noticed children struggling with fractions in their measurements, she offered help. She didn't push them if they were confused but planned to spend some time introducing them to beginning fractional concepts and notation. However, all of the children enjoyed the activity and stayed engaged until it was time for lunch. (See Figures 6–1 through 6–4.)

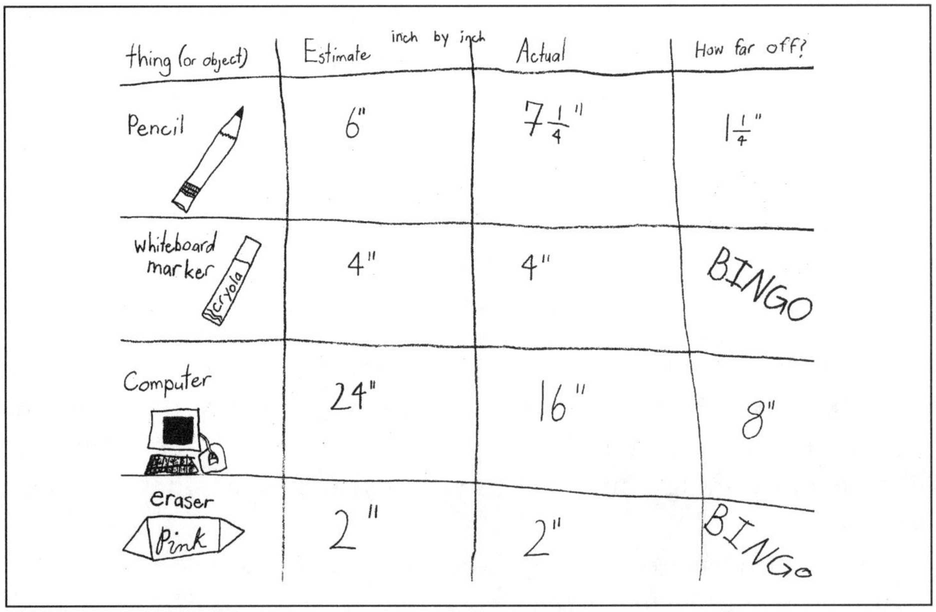

Figure 6–1: Julie's paper showed that she was able to estimate short lengths accurately.

thing (or object)	Estimate	Actual	How far off?
Pencil	6"	$7\frac{1}{4}$"	$1\frac{1}{4}$"
Whiteboard marker	4"	4"	BINGO
Computer	24"	16"	8"
eraser	2"	2"	BINGO

inch by inch

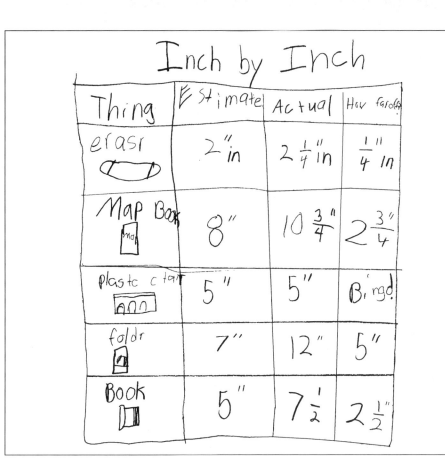

Inch by Inch

Thing	Estimate	Actual	How far off
erasr	2" in	$2\frac{1}{4}$" in	$\frac{1}{4}$" in
Map Box	8"	$10\frac{3}{4}$"	$2\frac{3}{4}$"
Plastc c tain	5"	5"	Bingo!
foldr	7"	12"	5"
Book	5"	$7\frac{1}{2}$"	$2\frac{1}{2}$"

Figure 6–2: Ana was one of the few students in the class who could deal with fractions other than halves. In her first measurements, she used both abbreviations, but then she correctly used just one in the rest of her paper.

Thing	Estimate	Acual	How far of?
Marsh Mcrnig Book	11"	$10\frac{1}{2}$	1"
Mikeroscope	7"	$8\frac{1}{2}$	1"
chair leg	15"	13"	2"
Andrew Sighn	$11\frac{1}{2}$	12"	1"
Bambboo fase	12"	9"	3"

Figure 6–3: Mattie was not able to figure differences correctly when fractions were involved.

Figure 6–4: Juanita
was pleased with her two
correct estimates.

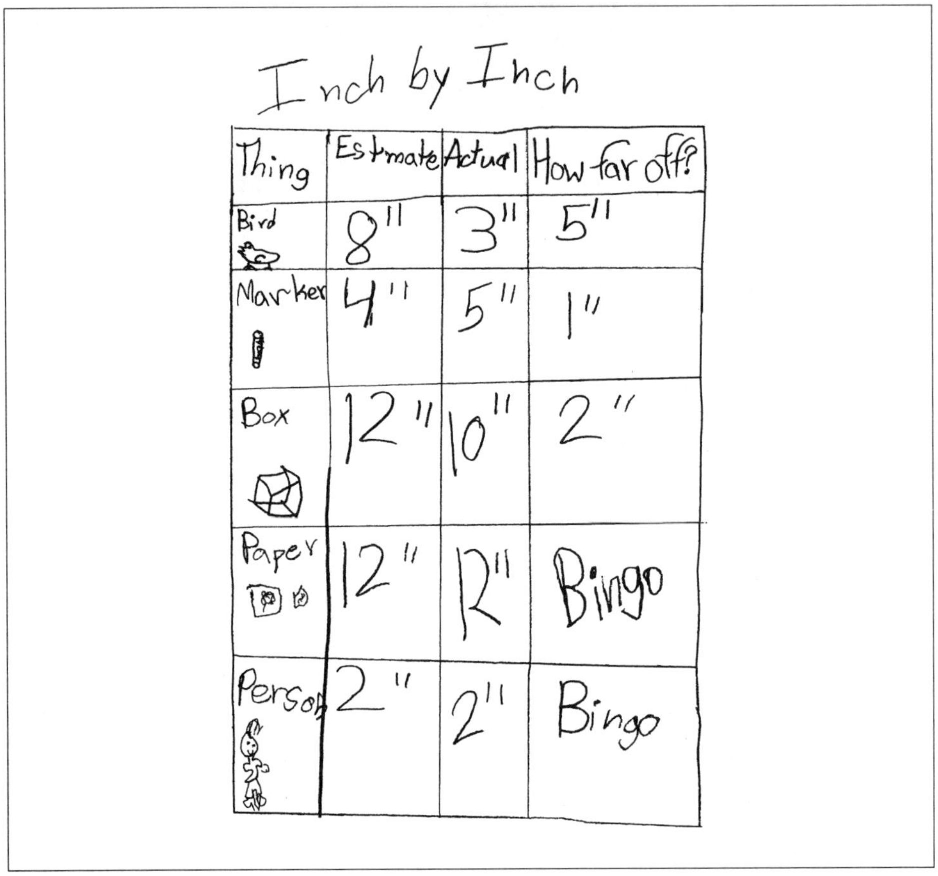

Inch by Inch

Thing	Estimate	Actual	How far off?
Bird	8"	3"	5"
Marker	4"	5"	1"
Box	12"	10"	2"
Paper	12"	12"	Bingo
Person	2"	2"	Bingo

The King's Commissioners

Taught by Marilyn Burns

Hilarious pictures complement *The King's Commissioners*, a tale by Aileen Friedman (1994b) about a king who has so many commissioners he loses track of how many there are. The King tells his commissioners to file into the throne room to be counted by his two Royal Advisors. One Royal Advisor counts by twos, and the other counts by fives, but the King is confused. It's up to the clever Princess to convince her father that there is more than one way to count. Marilyn Burns read the story to a class of second graders as part of an instructional unit on place value.

MATERIALS

Marilyn gathered the second graders on the rug and showed them the cover of *The King's Commissioners.*

"Who knows what a commissioner is?" she asked. Several of the students had ideas.

"He works for the king," Jason said, looking at the cover.

"He could work for the police, too," Mark added.

"I think that they do things in offices," Leslie said.

"Let's find out about the commissioners in this story," Marilyn said and began reading. The children giggled when Marilyn read the various jobs that the commissioners had—for flat tires, chicken pox, foul balls, and things that go bump in the night. They took delight in the vivid and humorous paintings, and they seemed sympathetic toward the confused King.

Marilyn read that the King wanted to know how many commissioners he had and was going to count them, one by one, as they came into the throne room and have the Royal Advisors keep track. On the page where the First Royal Advisor reports, "There are twenty-three 2s and 1 more," the illustration shows how the advisor made tally marks and circled groups of two. There are four rows of ten tally marks and a last row with the extra seven. After Marilyn read the rest of the text on that page, several children's shot their hands into the air, wanting to tell how many commissioners there were. Conversations broke out among some of the other children, also interested in figuring the total. Marilyn gave the children a few moments to talk and then called them back to attention.

"If you think you know how many commissioners there were," Marilyn said, "say the number softly in a whisper voice." Marilyn heard several different numbers. She invited the children to count along with her as she counted the tally marks by twos. Some faltered after twelve, others after fourteen or sixteen, but all were able to join in again when she reached the twenties. The teens often pose problems for children since the language pattern is irregular, while counting by twos from twenty on is easier.

"I knew it was forty-seven," Leslie said.

Marilyn then pointed out that there were ten tallies in each of the first four rows. "So we could count by tens," she said and did so, pointing to each of the four rows. When she reached forty, she counted the last row by saying, "Forty-two, forty-four, forty-six, and one more makes . . ." Marilyn hesitated so that the children could join in as she said, "Forty-seven."

The next page shows the Second Royal Advisor's tally marks. He has grouped them by fives and reports, "I got nine fives and two more." Several hands shot up, followed by others. Marilyn allowed time for the others to think and then had the children say the number in a whisper voice. She called on Tomo to explain how he got forty-seven.

Tomo explained, keeping track of the nine fives on his fingers, "I did five, ten, fifteen, twenty, twenty-five, thirty, thirty-five, forty, forty-five, and then two more is forty-seven."

"I did it the same way," Andrew said.

"Me, too," others added.

When the Princess had the King order the commissioners to line up in rows of ten, more of the children seemed sure that there were forty-seven in all.

After finishing the story, Marilyn reviewed with the children how the Royal Advisors and the Princess had counted the commissioners. She drew tally marks on the board the way the First Royal Advisor had drawn them on his chart, circling groups of two.

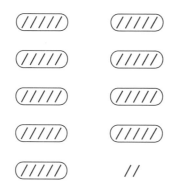

Underneath, Marilyn wrote:

23 2s and 1 more

"He counted by twos and added one more," she said. "He got forty-seven. Who can explain why his way to count made sense?" She gave several children the opportunity to explain.

"What about the Second Royal Advisor's counting plan? Does it make sense?" Marilyn then asked. She reproduced the Second Royal Advisor's chart on the board, circling groups of five.

Underneath, Marilyn wrote:

9 5s and 2 more

Then she said, "This advisor counted by fives. Who can explain how he got to forty-seven?" Again, she had several children explain.

Marilyn then said, "Even though the Princess didn't use tally marks, I can draw them to show how she counted." She drew tally marks on the board, circled groups of ten, and recorded underneath.

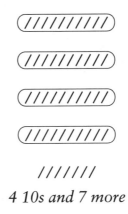

/////////

/////////

/////////

/////////

///////

4 10s and 7 more

After several children explained, Marilyn gave the students an assignment. She asked them each to write about why the Royal Advisors' and Princess's methods made sense. "You can use the ideas that others shared or ones of your own," she instructed. Then she wrote a

Figure 7–1: Annette explained how to count by twos, fives, and tens. She included an illustration of the Princess.

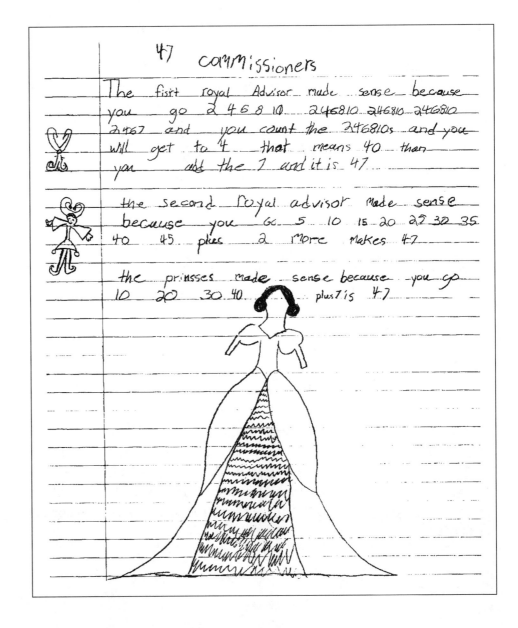

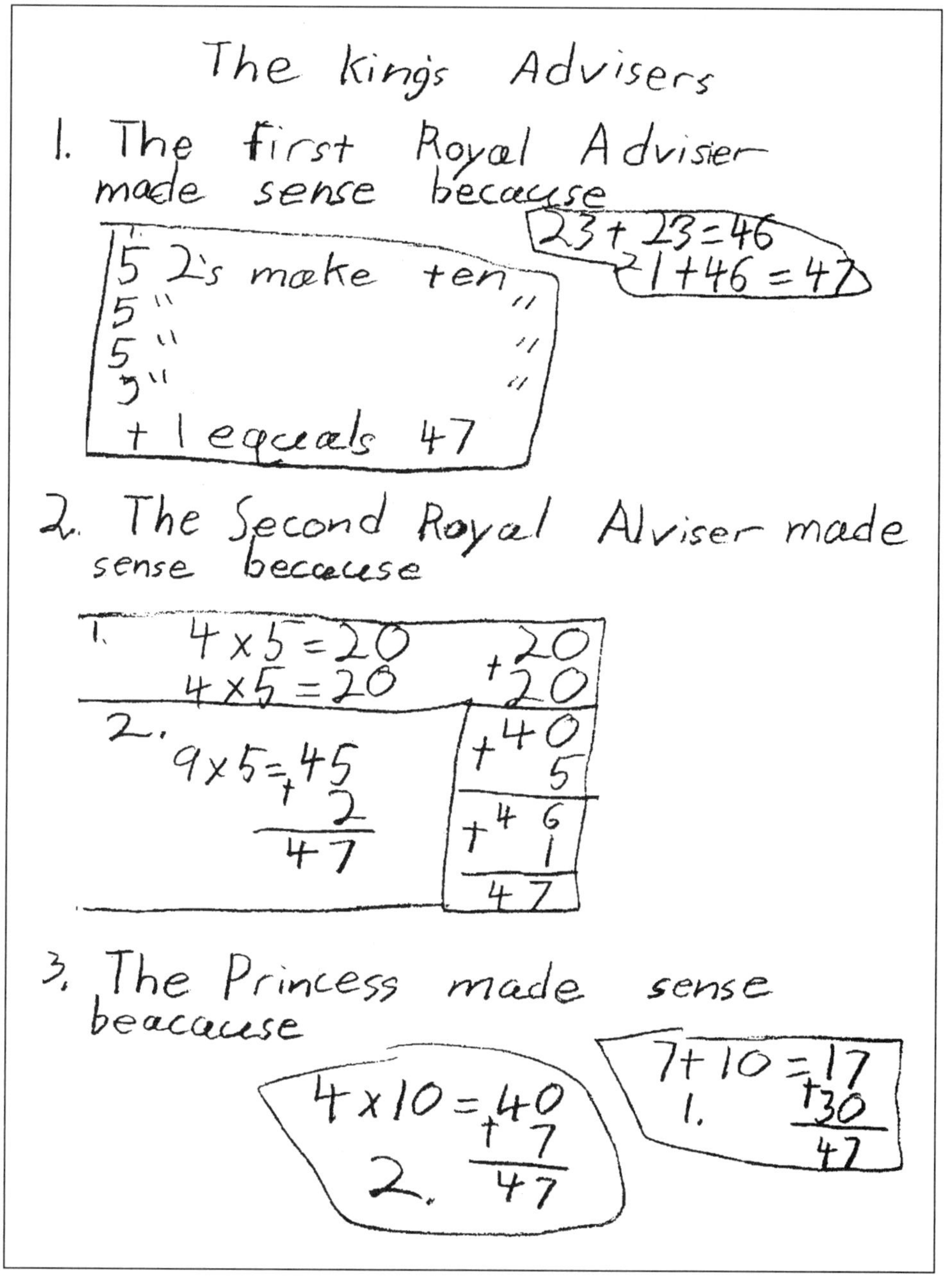

Figure 7–2: Alex calculated
in several ways.

The King's Advisers

1. The first Royal Adviser
made sense because

5 2's make ten "
5 "   "
5 "   "
3 "   "
+ 1 equals 47

23 + 23 = 46
1 + 46 = 47

2. The Second Royal Adviser made
sense because

1. 4 × 5 = 20   + 20
    4 × 5 = 20   + 20
2. 9 × 5 = 45   + 40
         + 2   5
         ___   + 46
          47   1
                       ___
                        47

3. The Princess made sense
because

4 × 10 = 40   7 + 10 = 17
       + 7   1.   + 30
2.   ___   ___
       47   47

prompt on the board to structure the students' writing:

1. *The First Royal Advisor made sense because* . . .

2. *The Second Royal Advisor made sense because* . . .

3. *The Princess made sense because* . . .

Figures 7–1 and 7–2 show how two students worked on this problem.
   (**Note:** Marilyn's experience with second graders is described more fully in *Teaching Arithmetic: Lessons for Introducing Place Value, Grade 2*, by Maryann Wickett and Marilyn Burns [2002]. See the References for more information.)

Little House in the Big Woods

Taught by Mary Petry-Cooper

Mary Petry-Cooper read *Little House in the Big Woods*, by Laura Ingalls Wilder (1932), to her third graders. A situation described in Chapter 10 presented a math problem involving fractions for her class to solve. Mary used the activity as a springboard for further teaching of fractions.

MATERIALS

Chapter 10 of *Little House in the Big Woods* takes place in summer, a time when people often go visiting. Sometimes, Ma lets Laura and Mary visit Mrs. Peterson, a neighbor. At the end of their visits, Mrs. Peterson always gives each of the girls a cookie. And the girls always consider how to share the cookies with Baby Carrie.

> Laura nibbled away exactly half of hers, and Mary nibbled exactly half of hers, and the other halves they saved for Baby Carrie. Then when they got home, Carrie had two half cookies, and that was a whole cookie.
>
> This wasn't right. All they wanted to do was to divide the cookies fairly with Carrie. Still, if Mary saved half her cookies while Laura ate the whole of hers, or if Laura saved half, and Mary ate her whole cookies, that wouldn't be fair, either.
>
> They didn't know what to do. So each saved half, and gave it to Baby Carrie. But they always felt that somehow that wasn't quite fair. (178–79)

Mary asked her third graders to think about a way to solve the cookie problem. "The children really identified with Laura and Mary and their cookie dilemma," Mary observed. "I was intrigued with the variety of solutions the children generated."

Most of the children suggested a way of dividing the cookies into parts. Their particular methods, however, differed. Several children divided each cookie into three parts so that Laura, Mary, and Baby Carrie would get two pieces each. Allison, for example, wrote: *If you had 3 kids and two cookie and did not no how to devide them heres how to do it: Devide the 2 cookies in to three part and then you would have 2 pieces for everybody.* (See Figure 8–1.)

Three children divided each cookie into nine segments and labeled six for each child. Jason, for example, wrote: *They could split the cookies like a pizza. So the all could get six.* (See Figure 8–2.)

Terri divided both cookies into halves and labeled one half for each of the three children. She then divided the remaining half into thirds and labeled each part. She wrote: *I took 2 cookies and split them in half for carrie and mary and Laura.* (See Figure 8–3.)

Ashley divided each cookie into fourths and labeled one part of each cookie for visitors. She wrote: *I think they should divide them into 4s. Then save the other two for company. But only if there's two people for company.*

Clinton wrote a long description of the story and then showed how to divide each cookie into sixths. He labeled four sections for each child. (See Figure 8–4.)

Some children, however, didn't divide the cookies but instead found social solutions to the problem. Antonio, for example, wrote: *They should save them an tale [until] there are six cookies so it will be evon.*

Chris's solution was brief and direct. He wrote: *Ask for three cookies, one for Carrie.*

How to Split Cookies
If you had 3 Kids and two cookie and did not no how to devide them heres how to do it: Devide the 2 cookies in to three part and then you would have 2 pieces for everybody.

Figure 8–1: Allison divided each cookie into thirds.

Figure 8-2: Jason divided each cookie into nine pieces and gave six to each child.

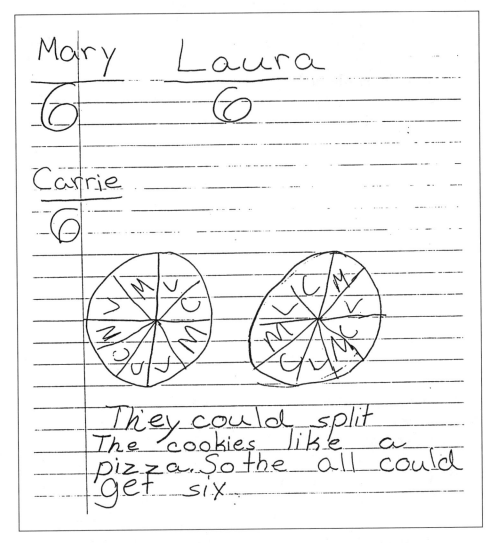

Mary   Laura

6   6

Carrie

6

They could split
The cookies like a
pizza. So the all could
get six

Figure 8-3: Terri's solution showed halves and sixths.

I took 2 cookies
and split them
in half for
carrie and mary
Laura

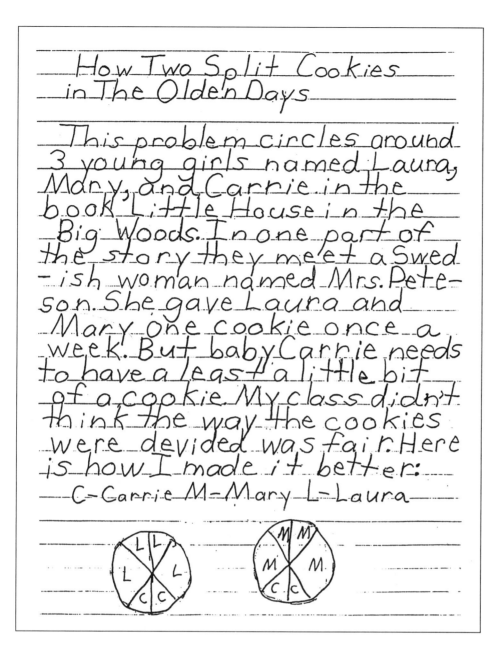

How Two Split Cookies in The Olden Days

This problem circles around 3 young girls named Laura, Mary, and Carrie in the book Little House in the Big Woods. In one part of the story they meet a Swed-ish woman named Mrs. Pete-son. She gave Laura and Mary one cookie once a week. But baby Carrie needs to have a least a little bit of a cookie. My class didn't think the way the cookies were devided was fair. Here is how I made it better:
C-Carrie M-Mary L-Laura

Timika was a bit more politic in a similar suggestion: *When you go to some bodys house and they give you and somebody else who went with you a cookie and you had a younger you can ask for another one.*

Melanie's idea was more expansive. She wrote: *Ask the little lady to give them five cookies one for mom for dad for carrie for mary and for lura.*

Mary planned to follow this problem with others that would focus her students on fractions.

Night Noises

Taught by Marilyn Burns

The main character in Mem Fox's book *Night Noises* (1992) is Lily Laceby, who is almost ninety years old and lives in a cottage with her dog, Butch Aggie. She drifts off to sleep one night but is awakened suddenly by strange noises made by her family and friends arriving for her surprise birthday party. Marilyn Burns read the story to a class of third graders and engaged the students in figuring out how many guests came to Lily Laceby's party and in what year she was born.

MATERIALS

The third graders paid close attention as Marilyn read *Night Noises* aloud. Several had comments after she finished the story.

"I liked how the little pictures on each page showed what she was dreaming," Julie said. Julie was referring to the small illustrations in the right corner of each spread that hint at Lily Laceby's dreams.

"I liked the words they used for the strange sounds," Priscilla added. In large type on each spread are "Crinch, Crunch," "Murmur, Mutter, Shhhh," and other words to describe the noises.

"I think she was nice what she said to Emily," Daria said. Emily was Lily's four-and-a-half-year-old great-great-grandchild. When she asked her great-great-grandmother if she were really ninety, Lily whispered to her, "Inside I'm only four-and-a-half, like you."

"Why do you think she told Emily that?" Marilyn asked.

"She was being nice to Emily," Daria said.

"Maybe she really feels that way inside, even though she's old on the outside," Isaac added.

"I don't get what this book has to do with math," Travon said, knowing that this was time for math.

"Oh, I know," Delia said. "I bet we get to figure out how many people came to the party."

"Yes, that's one of the problems I'd like you to solve," Marilyn said. Marilyn reread the two pages that describe who attends the party: "her two sons; her three daughters; her fourteen grandchildren; her thirty-five great-grandchildren; her great-great-grandchild, Emily, aged four-and-a-half; and her forty-seven friends."

"That's a lot to add," Warren said.

"Can we get paper?" Ana wanted to know.

"I'd like you to try to do the adding in your heads," Marilyn replied. "Listen as I read the first part about who came—two sons and three daughters."

"Five," several called out.

"Yes," Marilyn said, "but next time, don't call out your answer. Instead, raise a hand when you think you know. There were two sons, three daughters, and her fourteen grandchildren." A few children started to tell the answer, but Marilyn looked at them and put her finger to her lips to remind them not to blurt out. After a few moments, Marilyn asked them to say the answer in whisper voices.

"Nineteen," they chorused.

"Who can explain how you figured out that two sons, three daughters, and fourteen grandchildren add up to nineteen?" Marilyn asked.

Andrea explained, "I added two and three, and that's five. And then I added on the ten from the fourteen, and that made fifteen. And then I counted on four more to get nineteen." Marilyn recorded:

Andrea
$$2 + 3 = 5$$
$$5 + 10 = 15$$
$$15 + 4 = 19$$

Travon had another way to explain. He said, "I started the same— two and three are five. Then four more makes nine, and ten more makes nineteen." Marilyn recorded:

Travon
$$2 + 3 = 5$$
$$5 + 4 = 9$$
$$9 + 10 = 19$$

Warren explained, "I started with fourteen and counted five more. I got nineteen, too."

Julie then said, "I did fourteen plus two is sixteen and sixteen plus three is nineteen." Marilyn recorded Warren's and Julie's methods as she had done for the others.

"OK, let's continue," Marilyn said. "We know that nineteen came so far. Now we have to add on her thirty-five grandchildren. Think to yourself and raise a hand when you're ready with an answer." As the children were thinking, Marilyn wrote the problem horizontally on the board:

$$19 + 35$$

When almost all of the children had their hands raised, Marilyn again asked them to report together in whisper voices. This time Marilyn heard four different answers: fifty-five, fifty-four, fifty-two, and fifty-nine.

"Who wants to explain first?" Marilyn asked and then called on William. He had whispered fifty-nine, but when he explained, he wound up with the answer of fifty-four. He said, "I took ten from the nineteen and thirty-five plus ten is forty-five. Then I had nine more to add, so I did five first. Forty-five plus five is fifty. And fifty plus four is fifty-four." Marilyn recorded as William explained.

William
$$35 + 10 = 45$$
$$45 + 5 = 50$$
$$50 + 4 = 54$$

"Hey, that's not what I got before," William said. He thought for a minute. "But now I think that fifty-four is right," he concluded.

Daria explained her thinking next. She said, "First I added thirty-five plus five and that's forty. Then you take the five from the nineteen and you have fourteen more. So I did forty plus ten is fifty, and then all I had to do was add four. I got fifty-four, too."

Marilyn recorded:

Daria
$$35 + 5 = 40$$
$$19 - 5 = 14$$
$$10 + 40 = 50$$
$$50 + 4 = 54$$

Dawn imagined the problem written vertically and explained how she used the standard algorithm. "I put the nineteen under the thirty-five," she said, "and then I added five and nine. That's fourteen, so you write down the four and put a one on top of the three. Then you add and it's fifty-four." Marilyn recorded:

Dawn

$$\begin{array}{r} \overset{1}{3}5 \\ +\,19 \\ \hline 54 \end{array}$$

Marilyn didn't make reference to the wrong answers some had called out. Children often change their minds when they have a chance to rethink, and Marilyn didn't call their attention to their errors. Instead, she said, "OK, we know that fifty-four people came so far. Now we have to add on Emily, her great-great-grandchild. How many is that? Let's say it together in a whisper."

"Fifty-five!" the children whispered with confidence.

Marilyn then said, "We have one more number to add on—her forty-seven friends." She wrote the problem on the board, giving the children time to think.

$$55 + 47$$

More children were interested in reporting this time. The explanations given so far seemed to provide other students models for computing and the confidence to try. Marilyn recorded for each of the seven children who shared. Following are three of their methods.

Ana added the tens first—50 + 40. Then she added on the 5 from 55 and 5 of the 7 from 47 to get 100. Finally she added on the 2 left from 47. Marilyn recorded:

Ana

$$50 + 40 = 90$$
$$90 + 10 = 100$$
$$100 + 2 = 102$$

Delia added the ones first and then the tens and finally combined them. Marilyn recorded:

Delia

$$5 + 7 = 12$$
$$50 + 40 = 90$$
$$90 + 12 = 102$$

Isaac rounded 55 up to 60 and 47 up to 50. He added 60 and 50 by adding two 50s to get 100 and then adding on 10 more. Then he subtracted. Marilyn recorded:

Isaac
60 + 50 = 110
110 − 8 = 102

Marilyn then presented a different problem. "It's now the year two thousand three, and Lily is ninety years old. In what year was Lily Laceby born? How could we figure that out? Talk with your neighbor about this problem." As the children talked, Marilyn wrote on the board:

Lily Laceby turned 90 in 2003.
In what year was she born?

This problem was difficult for the children. Subtraction is typically more complicated for children than addition or multiplication, especially with larger numbers. About a third of the class was able to figure out the year. Isaac's explanation described how several children solved the problem. He figured out that if Lily were one hundred years old, then she would have been born in 1903. "But she's only ninety, so you have to add on ten years. So it's nineteen thirteen." Marilyn recorded:

Isaac
2003 − 100 = 1903
1903 + 10 = 1913

Antonio had another way to figure. "First I guessed nineteen-o-seven," he said, "but when I added on ninety, I got to nineteen ninety-seven. And that's six years ago, so I needed to add six more to nineteen-o-seven and got nineteen thirteen."

Antonio
1907 + 90 = 1997
2003 − 1997 = 6
1907 + 6 = 1913

Marilyn thought that these two methods were fairly sophisticated and was interested in what all of the children could do. She gave them a different problem to solve. "Oops," she said, "I didn't give you the right problem. This book wasn't written this year; it was written in nineteen eighty-nine, so that's when she had her birthday." Marilyn changed the problem on the board:

Lily Laceby turned 90 in 1989.
In what year was she born?

The children got out paper and pencils and went to work. Although the children tackled the problem with enthusiasm, it was out of reach for most of them, and their papers gave the clear message that they needed more work dealing with large numbers and ideas about place value. (See Figures 9–1 and 9–2.)

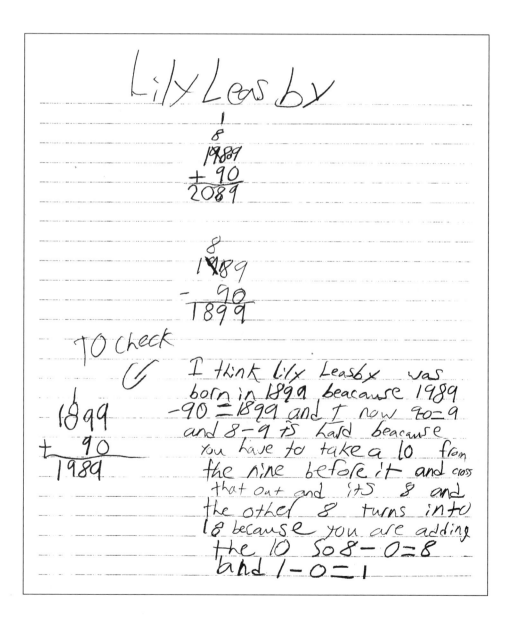

Figure 9–1: Daria was one of the few children who were able to solve the problem and explain their reasoning.

Figure 9–2: Andrea's paper showed her confusion both about the problem and about place value in general.

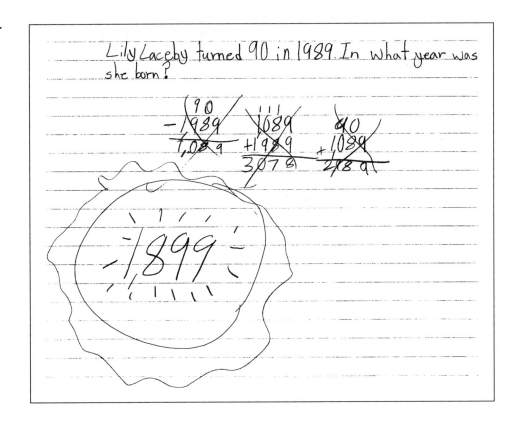

One Gorilla *and* One Duck Stuck

Taught by Marilyn Burns

Atsuko Morozumi's *One Gorilla* (1990) and Phyllis Root's *One Duck Stuck* (2001) are counting books that present the numbers from one to ten. In *One Gorilla*, a gorilla makes his way through jungles, gardens, and forests past two butterflies, three budgerigars, four squirrels, five pandas, six rabbits, seven frogs, eight fish, nine birds, and ten cats. In *One Duck Stuck*, two fish, three moose, four crickets, five frogs, six skunks, seven snails, eight possums, nine snakes, and ten dragonflies all try to help a duck stuck in a marsh. Marilyn Burns read *One Gorilla* to second graders and *One Duck Stuck* to third graders and involved each class with an addition problem.

MATERIALS

One Gorilla received the New York Times Best Illustrated Children's Book Award and *One Duck Stuck* was a National Council of Teachers of English notable children's book as well as a *Parents* Best Book of the Year. Marilyn read *One Gorilla* to second graders on the first day of school and used it to introduce them to problem solving. Also, she was interested in learning about the children's number sense and their ability to represent their ideas in writing. She read *One Duck Stuck* to third graders in December of the year and posed a similar problem. Marilyn found the children's papers useful assessments in both classes.

One Gorilla

Marilyn gathered the second graders on the rug. Since it was the first day of school, she spent some time getting them organized so that all children were sitting cross-legged and so that she could see each of their faces. When the children were settled, Marilyn showed them the cover of *One Gorilla* and read the title. Then she opened to the first spread and read, "Here is a list of things I love." Marilyn showed the children the illustration and gave them time to look at the details and report on what they noticed.

"He's got a banana in his toes," David said.

"He's going to eat lots of bananas," Lisa said.

"I had a banana for breakfast," Rebecca said.

"Me, too," several others chimed in.

"Do you see the flowers?" Marilyn asked to focus them back on the illustration. Several children commented on them. Larry pointed out the bananas growing at the top of the page.

Marilyn turned the page and there were "oohs" and "ahhs" when the children saw the field of tulips and daisies. "Can you find the two butterflies?" Marilyn asked. Since the butterflies are white and orange, the same colors used for the daisies, they weren't immediately obvious to the children, especially the smaller butterfly, which is about the same size as the daisy. The students got quiet as they searched the page.

"There's one!" Daniel exclaimed, noticing the larger butterfly. After a moment, Sarah spotted the other one.

"And can you see the gorilla?" Marilyn asked. The gorilla was easy to spot and many of the children immediately pointed to it.

The next spread shows the inside of a room and Marilyn invited the children to find the three budgerigars, one blue, one green, and one orange. This was easy for them to do.

"And can you see the gorilla?" Marilyn asked. In this illustration, the gorilla is outside the room, walking past the window, and it took a moment for all of the children to spot him.

As Marilyn continued through the book in this way, the children enjoyed searching for the creatures and finding the gorilla on each spread.

After showing the entire book to the class, Marilyn listed numerals on the board from *10* to *1*. "What animals from the book do you remember?" she asked the children. As students mentioned animals, Marilyn showed them the pages in the book where they appeared and wrote the names of the animals next to the appropriate numerals.

10 cats
9 birds

8 fish
7 frogs
6 rabbits
5 pandas
4 squirrels
3 budgerigars
2 butterflies
1 gorilla

Then Marilyn posed a math problem. She opened the book to the first page and again read, "Here is a list of things I love." Then she said, "Your job now is to figure out how many things the author loved altogether. I'm going to give each of you a piece of paper to work on. You can write or draw whatever will help you think about the problem. Then write your answer and explain how you figured."

Marilyn turned to the board and wrote:

He loved _____ things. I figured it by _____.

She read aloud what she had written and said to the class, "Write your name on your paper and also copy this down on your paper. Then work on solving the problem." Before distributing paper and sending the children back to their desks to begin their work, Marilyn said, "Raise your hand if you can explain the problem you're supposed to solve." About half of the children raised their hands and Marilyn called on two children to explain the problem.

She then showed the children the unlined paper she was going to distribute. "What are you supposed to write on the paper?" she asked. Again, Marilyn had volunteers explain.

She then sent the children back to their desks, dismissing them from the rug one by one as she gave them each a sheet of paper. The children got to work. The math period had the typical confusion of a first day at school. About half of the children were immediately engaged and went to work. Several children raised their hands for help. Several others began doing things that had nothing to do with the assignment—fiddling with things in their desks, drawing pictures that didn't relate to the problem, or wandering off to look for something. One boy had his head down and was gently sobbing, which he had been doing on and off all morning. Two boys argued about crayons.

As the children worked, Marilyn circulated, encouraging some children, refocusing others on the task, offering help, settling disputes, pushing for more explanations, and listening to children's ideas. She tried to comfort and understand the sobbing boy, who finally lifted his

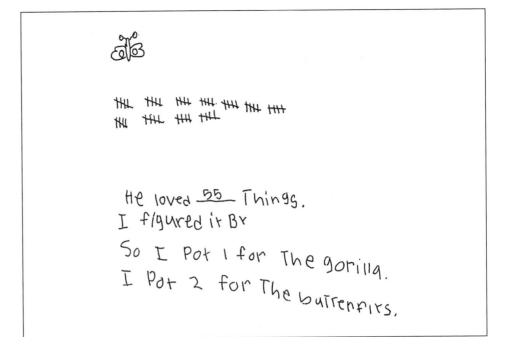

He loved __55__ Things.
I figured it Br
So I Pot 1 for The gorilla.
I Pot 2 for The butterflrs.

head and began to draw a dinosaur on his paper. Although it had nothing to do with the book, he said, "It's something I love."

Erin found the problem easy. She made tally marks and wrote: *He loved 55 things. I figured it by so I pot [put] 1 for the gorilla. I pot 2 for the butterflys.* She left the rest to the reader's imagination. (See Figure 10–1.) Several other children also drew lines or tally marks.

Jill was totally stuck. "These numbers are too big," she said. She had made lots of tally marks on her paper, following the lead of Erin and the others at her table, but the marks had no meaning for her. Marilyn told her that it was OK for her to explain that the numbers were too big because it was important for her to write what she really thought. Then Marilyn gave her a simpler problem to solve. She wrote on Jill's paper: *How many things can fly?* That was within Jill's reach. She wrote: *3 budgies, 9 birds, and 2 butterflys and 3 + 9 + 2 = 14.*

Daniel listed the numbers on his paper in the following order: *10, 9, 1, 8, 2, 7, 3, 6, 4, 5.* He wrote: *He loved 55 things. I added together to make 10s and then I added a 5. I did it in my head.* (See Figure 10–2.)

Beau drew dots in a triangular pattern, with one in the top row, two in the second row, and continuing to a tenth row with ten dots in it. He was pleased with the pattern and showed it to the others at his table, inspiring some of them to do the same. He wrote: *He loved 55 things. I figured it by dots.* (See Figure 10–3.) Several other children also drew dots to solve the problem.

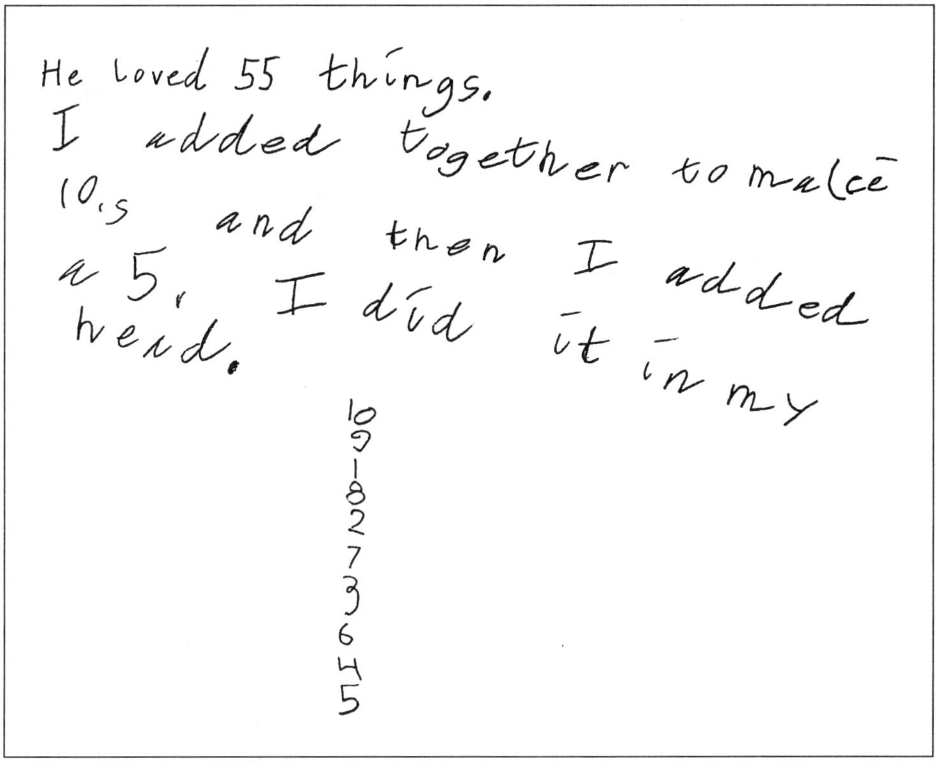

He loved 55 things.
I added together to make
10,s and then I added
a 5, I did it in my
head.

10
9
1
8
2
7
3
6
4
5

Figure 10–2: Combining tens allowed Daniel to figure in his head.

Figure 10–3: Beau was pleased with the pattern he made with dots.

Heloved55things,
Ifiguredit bydots,

Finally, Marilyn called all the children together and asked for volunteers to share their solutions. In this way the children had the chance to hear others' solutions and could see a variety of ways to organize their work on their papers.

One Duck Stuck

Marilyn gathered the third graders on the rug. Before starting to read *One Duck Stuck* to the class, Marilyn told them, "This is a counting book that I think poses an interesting math problem for you to solve. Also, please pay attention to the rich and vivid illustrations throughout the book and the wonderfully imaginative language that the author uses."

The children were quietly attentive as Marilyn read the story. Marilyn gave them time to enjoy the illustration on each spread, and they remained interested as different animals splished, plunked, and sloshed to help the one duck stuck in the muck. Several quietly cheered when it finally took all of the animals that appeared in the book, in a team effort, to rescue the duck.

At the end, several children made comments about the book. "I loved the rhymes," Andrea said.

"I was worried when the skunks came to help that they would smell bad," Warren added.

"They don't spray unless they're mad," Isaac said.

"I know what problem you're going to give us," Priscilla said.

"Well, let me explain the problem and see if this is what you thought," Marilyn replied. "The problem is to figure out how many animals came to help the one duck stuck in the muck." This problem is slightly different from the problem she had posed to the second graders for *One Gorilla*. In this problem, the children were to add the numbers from two to ten, while the second graders had to add the numbers from one to ten.

"I thought so!" Priscilla said.

"I think I already figured it out," William said.

William was about to tell the answer, but Marilyn stopped him. "Wait, William. Don't tell the answer just yet. In a moment, I'll ask everyone to go back to your desk and solve the problem in two different ways. So, William, one of your ways can be to explain what you did before you even left the rug. Solving a problem in two ways gives you a check on the answer."

"Can we draw pictures?" Julie wanted to know.

Marilyn responded, "Yes, as with all of your problem solutions, you should use words and numbers—and pictures if they help. But before you do any drawing, I'd like you to think about a way to solve the problem using numbers." Julie liked to draw and often got involved in making intricate drawings, and Marilyn had learned that Julie sometimes needed prodding to stay focused on the math task at hand.

"Do you need any other information from me before you start solving the problem?" Marilyn asked the class.

"Can you write the names of the animals on the board?" Daria asked.

"Yes, I can do that," Marilyn answered. "Is there anything else you need?" There were no other requests, so Marilyn dismissed the children and asked Travon and Melinda to pass out paper. As the children were getting settled and organized at their desks, she wrote on the board:

One Duck Stuck
How many animals came to help the duck?
Solve the problem in two ways.
2 fish
3 moose
4 crickets
5 frogs
6 skunks
7 snails
8 possums
9 snakes
10 dragonflies

Marilyn didn't ask them to copy on their papers what she had written on the board, but several children did. This was fine with Marilyn. She's learned that while copying from the board is a way for some children to settle and focus, others don't need to do this.

Marilyn circulated as the children got to work. She stopped at William's desk and asked him how he had solved the problem when they were on the rug. He said, "The other day I was adding up the numbers from one to ten, and I figured out that it was fifty-five. So I knew that the answer to this problem had to be one less. So I think it's fifty-four."

"How come you were working on that problem?" Marilyn asked. William shrugged, and Marilyn didn't push him to explain further. William loved math and often thought about mathematical problems and relationships. Instead, Marilyn asked, "Can you write down what you did to figure out the sum of the numbers from one to ten, and then think of another way to figure out this problem?" William nodded and got to work. (See Figure 10–4.)

Travon's strategy was to list the addends from 2 to 10 and then look for ways to combine them into tens. For example, he wrote $2 + 3 + 5 = 10$ and $6 + 4 = 10$. When Marilyn stopped by his desk, Travon had crossed out his work and was confused. "I know that fifty-seven is too much," he said, "but I can't see where I went wrong." Travon had checked with the others at his table and found out that they had all arrived at the answer of fifty-four.

Marilyn scanned his paper and noticed that he had used the three twice, resulting in an answer of fifty-seven instead of fifty-four. Marilyn helped Travon check off each of the addends he used, which helped him realize that he had used the three a second time. "Oh, I

Figure 10–4: In each of his solutions, William combined the addends, essentially doing it the same way both times with different representations. To add $9 + 5$, William added $10 + 5$ and then subtracted 1.

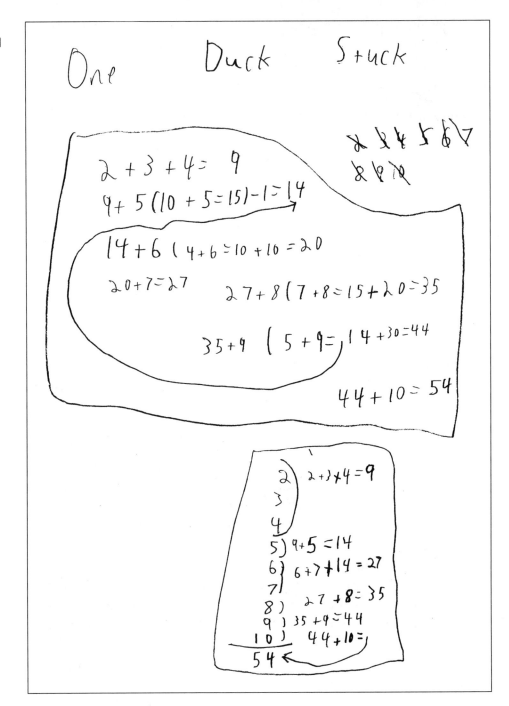

know," he said and wrote on his paper: *57 − 3 = 54 I used an extra three then I took it out.* "But I already crossed out my work," he said to Marilyn.

"That's OK," Marilyn replied. "I can read it just fine." Travon added to his paper: *I crossed it out, but it turned out to be ok.* Then he solved the problem another way, combining the addends differently to get the answer of fifty-four. (See Figure 10–5.)

Next Marilyn went to check on Juanita, who often struggled with math. She had copied the numbers and names of the animals from the board and below that had written: *I think 55. I was counting the*

Handwritten student work (Travon's paper):

One Deck stak

How many freinds helped him?. Solve the problel in two ways.

All numbers

- 1, 2 ✓
- 3 ✓ ✓
- 4 ✓
- 5 ✓
- 6 ✓
- 7 ✓
- 8 ✓
- 9 ✓
- 10 ✓

$2 + 3 + 5 = 10$
$3 + 7 = 10$
$6 + 4 = 10$
$8 + 9 = 17$
$10 + 0 = 10$
$57 - 3 = 54$

I used an extra three then I took it out

I crossed it out, but it turned out to be ok.

$2 + 3 + 4 + 5 + 6 + 7 + 8 + 9 + 10$

15
+10
+12
+27
54

---

animals but I still got 55. Juanita was just starting to draw the animals. Marilyn asked Juanita to join her at the back table. Juanita did so happily. Marilyn often worked with Juanita when the class was involved in solving problems, and Juanita responded well. She was an eager student but struggled with getting started on math problems. When they were at the back table, Marilyn told Juanita, "I was just talking with Travon, and he had a really interesting way to figure out the answer. He looked for tens in the numbers you have to add. For example, he noticed that four plus six is ten." Juanita nodded. "How about we look for tens together," Marilyn said.

"Should I write that one down?" Juanita asked. Marilyn nodded and Juanita wrote *4* and *6* vertically, added a plus sign, drew a line, and wrote *10*.

Marilyn asked Juanita to make a check mark next to the 4 and 6 in her list and then asked, "Can you find any other numbers that add to ten?" Juanita nodded and added *8 + 2* and then *7 + 3*, carefully recording each. The numbers 9, 10, and 5 were left. Juanita added 9 + 10 to get 19, and then added the 5 onto one of the sums of 10 to get 15. Finally she combined two 10s, 15, and 19 and got 54. Juanita wrote: *But when I was doing adding I got 54 but I thought it was 55.* (See Figure 10–6.)

Figure 10–6: Juanita struggled with math and completed only one method, but Marilyn decided that this was sufficient for this assignment.

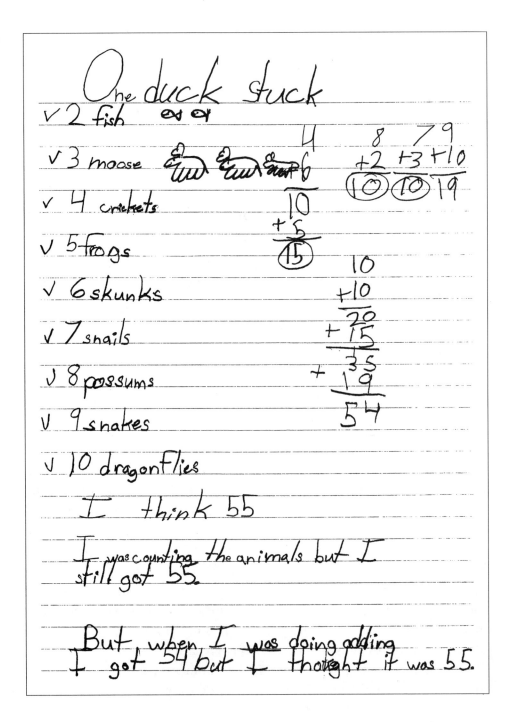

Math and Literature, Grades 2–3

As Juanita was finishing her paper, several children lined up to show Marilyn their work. She told those who had completed the assignment to return to the work they were doing before math—practicing their cursive. To a few, she made additional suggestions for their papers.

Marilyn then circulated again around the room and went to check on Julie. She found her intently focused on drawing the animals. On another sheet of paper she had listed the numbers in a column, added them, and recorded the incorrect answer of 48. There was no evidence of her thinking on that paper. Also, unlike Travon, she hadn't checked with the others at her table, but instead had plunged into drawing. Marilyn interrupted Julie and asked, "Can you explain to me how you added the numbers?"

Julie thought for a moment and then said, "First I added two and three, and that gave me five. Then I added four and five, and that gave me nine."

Marilyn asked, "Can you record as you explain so that I can be sure I understand what you did?" Marilyn was interested in seeing if recording would help Julie correct her answer for herself.

Julie did all of the additions vertically. She first wrote 5 (from adding two and three), then underneath 9 (from adding four and five), and then the answer of 14. "I know that one," she said.

Julie crossed out the numbers she had just added and then said, "I'll add on the nine next." She wrote 09 underneath the 14 and added to get 23. Marilyn was curious about why Julie wrote the zero before the nine, but she didn't question her at this time since Julie was concentrating on the problem so intently.

Julie crossed out the 09 and said, "I'll do six and seven next." She wrote 13 underneath the 23 and added to get 36. For each addition, Julie was careful to add the ones first and then the tens. Julie added the 8 next, again writing 08 as she had done with the 09. The subtotal was now 44, and adding the remaining number, 10, brought it to 54. Julie looked at the 48 she had previously written as the answer.

"Which answer do you think is right?" Marilyn asked her.

"I'm not sure," Julie said. "Oh, I know. I'll do it another way." Julie then combined the numbers differently, recording to the left of her list of addends and again arriving at fifty-four. She erased the 48 she had previously written and replaced it with 54. (See Figures 10–7 and 10–8.)

Marilyn then asked Julie another question. She pointed to where Julie had written 09 and 08 for 9 and 8. "Why did you write zeroes before the nine and the eight?" she asked.

"They look better when they line up two by two," Julie responded. It seemed that Julie's interest in art also affected her mathematical representations.

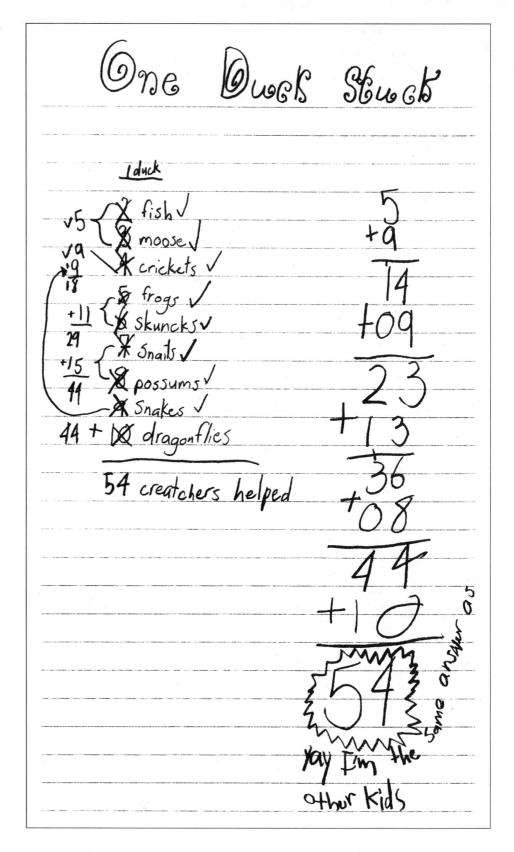

Figure 10–7: After Julie arrived at the correct answer, she wrote: Yay I'm the same answer as other kids.

The handwritten work shows:

One Duck Stuck

1 duck

√5 { fish ✓
√9 { moose ✓
√9 crickets ✓
18
+11 { frogs ✓
29 { skuncks ✓
+15 { snails ✓
44 possums ✓
snakes ✓
44 + dragonflies

54 creatchers helped

5
+9
14
+09
23
+13
36
+08
44
+10
54

Yay I'm the same answer as other kids

Figure 10–8: Julie's second paper showed her interest in and talent with drawing.

Almost all of the students solved the problem by adding combinations of the addends and then adding the subtotals. (See Figure 10–9 on the following page.)

The third graders' papers differed from the papers of the second graders who solved the problem from *One Gorilla*. Most of the second graders relied on drawing the animals and counting them. However, only a few of the third graders drew the animals to find the answer; most found two ways to arrive at the answer numerically.

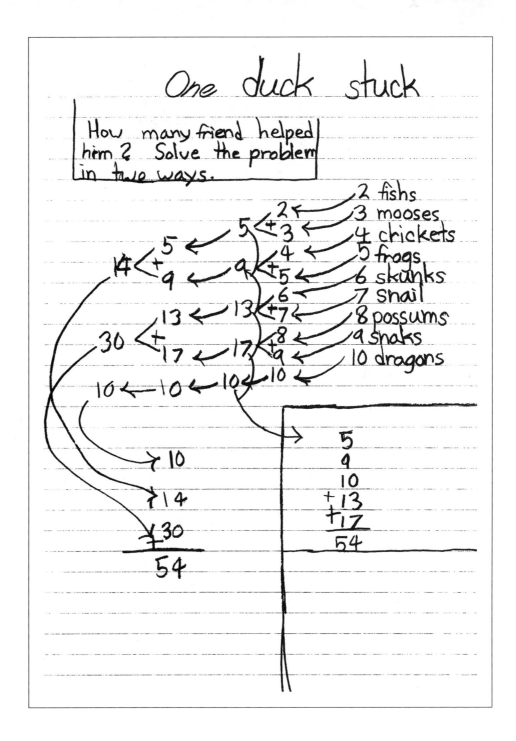

One Hundred Hungry Ants

*Taught by Stephanie Sheffield,
Marilyn Burns, and Dee Uyeda*

Elinor J. Pinczes's book *One Hundred Hungry Ants* (1993) tells the story of one hundred ants that are hurrying to a nearby picnic. Marching in single file seems too slow to the littlest ant, who suggests they travel in two rows of fifty. When that also seems too slow, the littlest ant suggests four rows of twenty-five. The ants scurry to reorganize several more times and finally arrive at the picnic in a 10-by-10 array, too late for food! The lively marching verses delight children, and the story is useful for giving second and third graders informal experience with multiplication and division. Stephanie Sheffield and Marilyn Burns read the book to two second-grade classes, and Dee Uyeda read it to a third-grade class.

MATERIALS

As Stephanie read *One Hundred Hungry Ants* aloud to a class of second graders, several of the students made comments.

"He sure is bossing them around," Reed said.

"All this stopping is slowing them down; they would get there faster if they just kept on walking," Scott commented.

"There goes the rabbit with a sandwich," Audrey noticed.

Before long, most of the students guessed that no food would be left by the time the ants got to the picnic.

After Stephanie read the book, she initiated a discussion about the different ways the littlest ant arranged his friends. "How did they start out?" she asked.

"First they were in one line of one hundred," Thalia said. On the board Stephanie wrote: *1 line of 100.*

"What did the littlest ant do first?" Stephanie asked. Audrey raised her hand.

"It put them in two lines of fifty," she said. Stephanie recorded that as well.

Antonio started to tell Stephanie what to write next. "Then he made twenty-five rows of four," he said.

"No, that's not right! He means four rows of twenty-five," Mark shouted.

"It's the same thing!" Hassan said.

Other children called out, "No, it's not!" "Yes, it is!" The commutative nature of multiplication is a valuable concept for children to have, and the students' disagreement gave Stephanie an opportunity to help build their understanding.

"Let's think about this," Stephanie said. "How can we figure out if these two sentences are the same?" She wrote on the board: *25 rows of 4* and *4 rows of 25.*

"We could act it out," Judy suggested.

"How many children would we need?" Stephanie asked.

"One hundred!" Karen said. The children decided the idea wasn't practical. They were stumped about how to proceed.

"What makes this a hard problem?" Stephanie asked.

"We don't have enough kids to act it out," Kendra answered.

"How about a simpler problem?" Stephanie said and crossed out the 5s in the phrases so that they read 4 rows of 2 and 2 rows of 4.

"Can you act this out?" Stephanie asked.

"Now we can do it!" Thalia said.

Stephanie called on eight students to come to an open part of the room and line up in four rows of two. As they stood there, the rest of the students walked around them and talked about what they saw.

"It's like two rows, if you walk around them," Hassan said. "I still think they're the same because it's the same eight people."

"It doesn't matter, unless they have to walk through a tunnel," Jed commented. "Then they'd better be in four rows of two."

Stephanie wasn't sure the children were transferring this example to four rows of twenty-five and twenty-five rows of four, but they seemed satisfied. So she had them all sit down, and they continued discussing the book. "What was the next way the littlest ant arranged its friends?" Stephanie asked.

Wally answered, "Five rows of twenty. It's a pattern. One row, two rows, three rows . . . no, wait. Why didn't he put them in three rows?"

"Maybe he didn't think of it," Kendra suggested. Stephanie watched the students' faces and could tell that this was a question that intrigued them.

"I don't think it would work," Karen said.

When Stephanie chose this book to use with her class, she intended to try what Marilyn Burns reported she had done with second graders. After reading the book, Marilyn had asked students to choose a new number of ants and think about all the ways they could arrange themselves into rectangles to get to the picnic. She had given them a choice of numbers of ants to consider—twelve, twenty-four, or sixty. Stephanie had planned to do this as well.

However, because of the responses to Wally's question, she changed her plan. She has learned that what she plans for a lesson might not be what actually occurs. While it's important to have some idea about the mathematical potential in a book and plan for a lesson, it's also important to stay flexible and follow children's leads when they offer the opportunity to look at a mathematical idea. Stephanie decided to pose a problem based on Wally's question and see what the students would do with the problem of dividing one hundred into three equal groups.

"Could the littlest ant have arranged its friends into three equal lines?" Stephanie asked. "I'd like you to try to answer that question and write down your solution. If you decide the answer is yes, tell me how many ants would be in each line. If your answer is no, explain why it isn't possible. I want you to explain your thinking as clearly as possible so that someone reading your paper will know just what you were thinking. Don't worry about erasing parts that don't work out. I'm interested in all of your thinking, including your mistakes. You can use words, pictures, numbers, or any combination of these to solve the problem."

Whenever Stephanie gives directions about a problem to solve, she asks several students to repeat them. This gives her a way to be sure they understand what to do. It also provides those students who are not strong in auditory skills another chance to get the directions.

"OK, who can explain in your own words what to do?" Stephanie asked.

Reed explained, "The littlest ant wants to know if he can put all one hundred ants into three rows with no leftovers. We have to tell if he can do that or not."

"Who has another way to explain the problem?" Stephanie asked.

"You have to line up one hundred ants in three lines," Judy said.

"Anything else?" Stephanie prompted.

"We have to write down everything we think," Karen added.

"And we can draw pictures," Audrey said.

Some children chose partners, while others chose to work alone. Wally and Hassan made one hundred tally marks, then drew a box and divided it into three parts. They transferred the one hundred tally marks to the box, carefully writing them one by one in each section and crossing them off as they did so. Other students, such as Jed and

Figure 11–1: After using
tally marks, Scott explained
why the problem was
impossible.

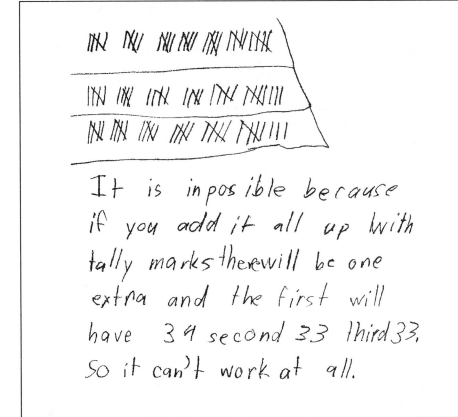

It is inposible because
if you add it all up with
tally marks therewill be one
extra and the first will
have 34 second 33 third 33,
So it can't work at all.

Thalia, made tally marks in groups of three, counted to one hundred, and found there was one extra tally. Scott used tally marks as well. (See Figure 11–1.)

Alex and Jake started with marks in groups of three but quickly moved to writing addition problems to see if they could get to one hundred by adding a number to itself three times. They started with $3 \times 12 = 36$, then tried $30 + 30 + 30 = 90$, $32 + 32 + 32 = 96$, $33 + 33 + 33 = 99$, and finally $34 + 34 + 34 = 102$. At this point, they decided it was impossible and wrote $34 + 33 + 33 = 100$ to prove their thinking. (See Figure 11–2.)

Audrey, Angie, and Jane each made long lines of three marks to resemble the ants while counting to one hundred. They knew it was impossible when the lines didn't come out even.

Reed wrote the numbers from 1 to 100, arranging them in three columns. He wound up with 100 as an extra in the first column. (See Figure 11–3.)

As students shared their solutions, they listened to one another and seemed interested in the ways others had solved the problem. They were all convinced by their own solutions that it wasn't possible, but hearing other approaches helped verify their thinking and introduced them to other approaches.

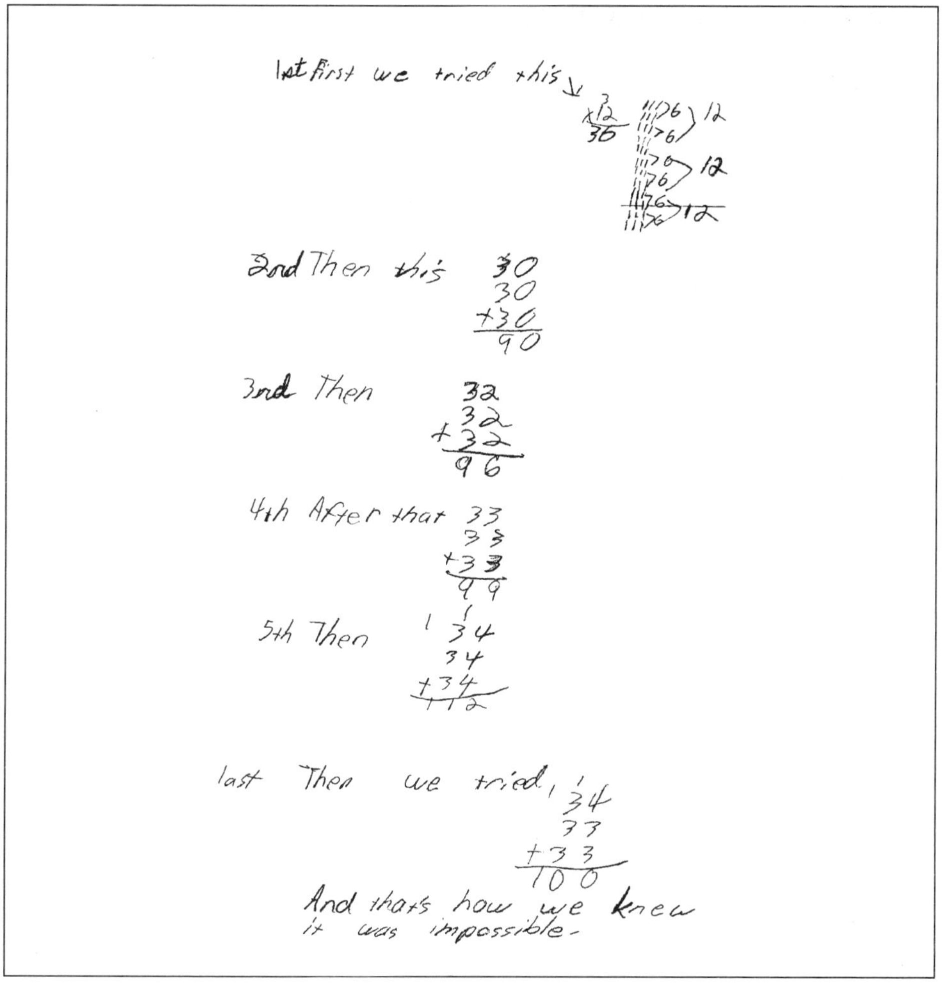

Figure 11–2: Alex and Jake tried adding a number to itself three times to get to one hundred.

Figure 11–3: Reed found the "answer impossible" after writing the numerals from 1 to 100 in three columns.

A Different Lesson with Second Graders

When Marilyn Burns used *One Hundred Hungry Ants* with second graders, she reported that after reading the story a few times, she posed a problem: "Suppose only ten ants were going to the picnic." Marilyn drew a row of ten circles on the board. "If the ants reorganized into two rows, how many would be in each row?" she asked. This problem was easy for the children, and Marilyn drew two rows with five circles in each to illustrate the answer.

"What about if the ants tried to get into three rows?" Marilyn then asked. "Could they get into three rows and have the same number in each?" Even though she hadn't talked about having the same number of ants in each row, the children seemed to infer this constraint from the story.

"Maybe there would be just four in each row," Leilani volunteered.

Marilyn tested Leilani's suggestion, drawing three rows with four circles in each. The children counted, found there were twelve circles in all, and agreed it wouldn't work. "Three groups of four make twelve," Marilyn said and wrote $3 \times 4 = 12$ next to her drawing. Marilyn reported that recording like this is the sort of incidental way she tries to connect mathematical symbolism to children's thinking.

"Put three in each," Ross suggested next. Marilyn drew three rows, each with three circles.

"That's not enough," Alex said impatiently. "It won't work." Alex had a keen number sense. Marilyn had the children count the circles and then recorded on the board: $3 \times 3 = 9$.

"Alex is right," Marilyn said. "You can't put ten ants into three rows and have the same number in each row. What about four rows?" She investigated this idea with the class in the same way, drawing and labeling to verify that it wasn't possible. Then they tried five rows and saw that it worked with two in each.

Marilyn stopped and wrote a chart on the board:

10 Hungry Ants

1 row	*10*
2 rows	*5*
3 rows	*can't*
4 rows	*can't*
5 rows	*2*
6 rows	
7 rows	
8 rows	
9 rows	
10 rows	

"A chart like this is one way to keep track of what we're finding," she told the class. "But instead of finishing this problem together, you're each going to try one on your own."

Marilyn gave the children directions. "First, decide the number of ants you'd like to explore," she said. "Then set up a chart as I did, but write your number in the title where I wrote ten." She erased the 10, replaced it with a dash, and erased the answers she had written so far.

"You can choose one of these numbers," Marilyn continued and wrote *12, 24,* and *60* on the board. "I like giving students options like this," Marilyn reported, "because their choices give me insights into their comfort with numbers. But I also wanted to have several children working on the same number so we could have group discussions about the results."

"Can we pick our own number?" Seiji asked. Seiji was fascinated by large numbers.

"If you want to choose a number that is different from one of these three," Marilyn responded, "then you have to tell me first, and I'll let you know if it's OK." This decision gave her the chance to converse with children about their thinking.

During the rest of the math period, children set up their papers and negotiated number choices with Marilyn. Alex wanted to explore five hundred, and she readily agreed. Seiji asked for two hundred, and she told him that was fine.

David, Sheryl, and Sally were at the same table. "Can we all do fifty?" they asked. Marilyn agreed, thinking they could relate this number to the story of one hundred ants. Jane, also at their table, was already beginning work on sixty.

When Marilyn looked at the students' papers, she noticed that of the 24 children in the class, 5 chose to explore twelve, 8 chose twenty-four, 3 chose sixty, and 6 had negotiated other choices. Two children, Lynn and Darius, had chosen their own numbers—fifteen and thirty.

Most of the children didn't have time to finish working on the problem. The next day Marilyn reviewed the activity and had the students return to work. Three children changed their numbers; two of them changed from twenty-four to twelve, and one changed from sixty to twelve. "Changing their minds was fine with me," Marilyn reported. "I was pleased to see them thinking about appropriate choices."

As children finished their work, Marilyn had them find someone else who was also finished and explain their solutions to each other. In this way, children had opportunities to compare the results from different numbers. (See Figures 11–4 through 11–6.)

Figure 11–4: Emily used
tiles to figure out the
solutions.

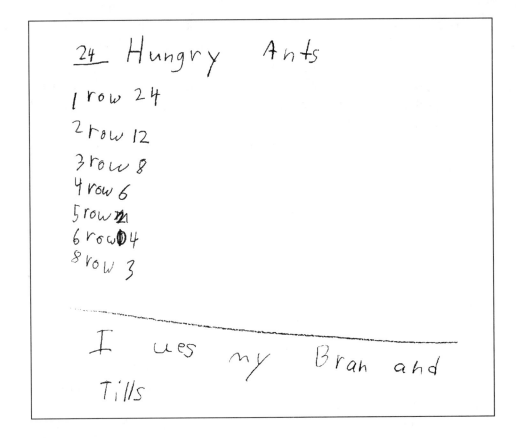

Figure 11–5: Kendall was
one of eight children who
chose to explore twelve.

Math and Literature, Grades 2–3

Presenting a Problem to a Third-Grade Class

Dee Uyeda read *One Hundred Hungry Ants* to her third graders after they had been studying multiplication and division. She asked the children to choose a number to explore, but she didn't give any suggestions or set any limits. Also, she integrated a writing experience into the math assignment, asking the children to write stories similar to *One Hundred Hungry Ants* but using their own numbers and any other characters or settings that they would like. Dee told the children that they could work individually or in pairs.

"There are two parts you have to do and one more you can choose to do if you like," Dee explained. The two required parts were for children to write the story and to explain how they figured out the mathematics. The optional part was to draw pictures to illustrate their stories.

The different characters the children chose included swarming bees, migrating birds, elephants, mice, snakes, and bookworms. Several pairs chose 120, the smallest number chosen; the other numbers included 150, 160, 200, 400, and 800. (See Figures 11–7 and 11–8.)

Figure 11–7: Marianne and Annie explained how they did the math for lining up four hundred mice.

How We Fugurgred it Out.

We Took half of 4. It is 2 and half of two is 1 but now we are working with hundres so 100. Half of 100 is 50 and half of 50 is 25. 25 is not an even number. So we took 16 lines and of 25 and mad it in to 20 lines of 20 half of 20 is 10.

400
200
100
50
25
20
10

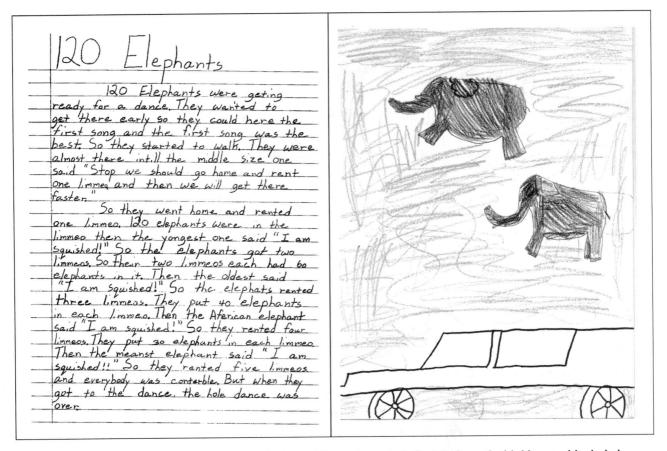

120 Elephants

120 Elephants were geting ready for a dance. They wanted to get there early so they could here the first song and the first song was the best. So they started to walk. They were almost there. intll the middle size one said "Stop we should go home and rent one limmeo and then we will get there faster."

So they went home and rented one limmeo. 120 elephants were in the limmeo then the yongest one said "I am squished!" So the elephants got two limmeos. So their two limmeos each had 60 elephants in it. Then the oldest said "I am squished!" So the elephants rented three limmeos. They put 40 elephants in each limmeo. Then the African elephant said "I am squished!" So they rented four limmeos. They put 30 elephants in each limmeo. Then the meanst elephant said "I am squished!!" So they rented five limmeos and everybody was conterble. But when they got to the dance. the hole dance was over.

Figure 11–8: Erica and Jamie wrote about elephants and limousines, explained their math thinking, and included an illustration.

Not all of the children found all of the possible ways to line up objects. For example, Joanne and Celia's story was titled *150 Hungry Book Worms*. They wrote:

Off to the library went 150 book worms. In a strat line. Down the street. "Stop" said the tallest book worm. "were going too slow the library will close befor we get there. Split up into three lines of 50." It took them a long time. Off to the library. "Stop" said the tallest one. "Well neer get there in time. The library is going to close. Split up into 6 lines of 25." It took them a long time. Off to the library. "Stop" said the tallest one. "There closed." 149 book worms chashed the tallest book worm all the way home. "It's not my failt you took too long to get in line."

Only One

Taught by Stephanie Sheffield

In *Only One*, Marc Harshman (1993) poetically assigns numbers to familiar things. He begins, "There may be a million stars, But there is only one sky. There may be 50,000 bees, But there is only one hive. There may be 500 seeds, But there is only one pumpkin." The next page skips down to one hundred, then to twelve, and the following pages count down to one, each time contrasting a group with a single object. Stephanie Sheffield used this unique counting book to give a class of second graders the opportunity to discuss things that come in groups of various sizes.

MATERIALS

Stephanie gathered a class of second graders on the rug and showed them the cover of *Only One*.

"I have a book to share with you today that has some interesting mathematical ideas," she began. "But first, let me tell you about the unusual illustrations. They're called collagraphics." Stephanie read the description on the copyright page that explains how the collages in the book were made. The children listened with interest. Then Stephanie read the book to them.

"What did you notice about this book?" she asked after she'd finished reading it.

"There was only one sentence on each page," Kendra said.

"Every page has the same words, *only one*," Judy said.

"The numbers get smaller," Jed said.

"Yes," Wally agreed, "they started out really big and jumped down fast."

"Let's go back and look," Stephanie said. "The first page says, 'There may be a million stars, but there is only one sky.' The next number mentioned is fifty thousand."

Jed raised his hand. "If they went down by ones, the next number would be nine hundred ninety-nine thousand nine hundred and ninety-nine. The book would be too long."

"But it did start to go down by ones," Karen said.

"Let's reread the book to find out where it starts counting down by ones," Stephanie suggested. After fifty thousand came five hundred, then one hundred, and then twelve. From twelve on, the numbers decreased by one. When Stephanie read the page that says, "There may be 10 cents, But there is only one dime," Nikki was eager to comment.

"A dime is the same as ten cents, and ten pennies is a dime," she said.

Stephanie turned back to the previous page and reread it: "There may be eleven cows, but there is only one herd." She then said, "I think the dime page has to be the page about ten, but the herd page doesn't have to be about eleven. Why do I think this?"

Alex's hand shot up. He said, "A herd can be any number, but a dime is only ten pennies." Others agreed.

Most of the pages in the book used words like *herd, sky,* and *merry-go-round,* which might be used with several different numbers. But some pages had words that were number-specific, like *dime* and *trio.* Stephanie wrote *Herd* and *Dime* on the board to title two columns and focused the children on each of the other pages in the book. As they talked about each page, she listed the topic in the correct column. The children were fascinated to look at the pages again and see which kind of page each one was.

Some pages created a good deal of discussion. For instance, the page that reads, "There may be 9 players, But there is only one team" pictures a baseball team. Some students thought this made it a Dime page, but Scott pointed out that soccer teams have eleven players and basketball teams have five. The class finally agreed to put *team* in the Herd column.

Next, Stephanie asked the students if they would like to write a class *Only One* book. They responded enthusiastically. To get them started, Stephanie suggested they first think about things that might come in large groups. After a few moments, several children raised their hands. Stephanie called on Karen.

"There may be ten thousand people, but there is only one crowd," she said.

"Which column should that go in?" Stephanie asked.

"Herd!" the children answered in a chorus.

Judy raised her hand. "There may be a hundred dogs, but there is only one Clifford the big red dog."

Alex protested. "That won't work. Clifford is just another dog. It's not like a herd or a dime." Alex had trouble expressing what bothered him, but he knew somehow that this idea was different.

Stephanie went back to the page with the herd of cows. "On this page a herd is made of eleven cows," she said. She turned the page. "Here, a dime is worth the same as ten pennies. Judy, which of these pages is your idea like?"

"I'm not sure," she said. Stephanie told her to keep thinking and said she'd get back to her in a bit.

The children's ideas came as fast as Stephanie could write them down. For each suggestion, she asked whether the idea was like the herd or the dime. The children were interested and very involved in the discussion. Now and then there was a dispute, but they were able to talk it through. Also, Judy decided to change her example. Some of the ideas in the Herd column were tanks (one army), jets (one airport), and pencils (one pencil box). Some of the ideas in the Dime column were months (one year), letters (one alphabet), and states (one United States of America).

The list on the board proved helpful when they talked about how to organize the class book. They decided to start with large numbers, skip down to twelve, and then count down from twelve to one, the way the book does. The students had ideas for most of the numbers, but they were missing a few. For eleven, for example, they had nothing listed on the board. Jed jumped up.

"I know, we can change the one about the tanks and the army!" he said.

"Never!" Mark said vehemently. It was his idea for the number 550, and he didn't want it changed. Stephanie pointed out that eleven tanks might not make a great army, and Jed turned his attention to finding a different idea.

Hassan pointed to the Herd column. "Those are the ones that could be another number," he said. The class decided to use the jets-and-airport idea for eleven and moved on.

Each child claimed an idea to write and illustrate, and the book was on its way. (See Figures 12–1 and 12–2.) Most children were interested in writing and illustrating the sentences they had contributed. Three students were so interested in the activity that they went on to write their own *Only One* books.

Figure 12–1: These pages from the class book were Herd examples.

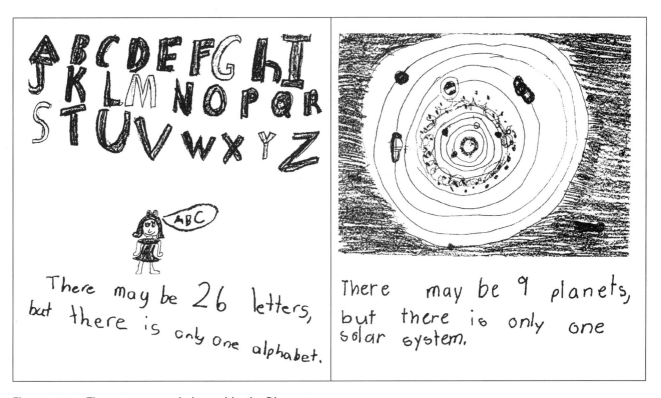

Figure 12–2: These two pages belonged in the Dime category.

P. Bear's New Year's Party

Taught by Stephanie Sheffield

"You are cordially invited to P. BEAR'S NEW YEAR'S PARTY! (Formal dress required.)" So begins the charmingly simple counting book *P. Bear's New Year's Party*, by Paul Owen Lewis (1989). P. Bear sends party invitations to his best-dressed friends. At one o'clock, the first guest arrives; at two o'clock, two more guests arrive. Every hour after that, the number of guests that arrives matches the hour on the clock. The last page of the book asks the question, "How many guests came to the party?" Stephanie Sheffield posed this problem to both second and third graders, providing them the opportunity to use addition or, if they were able, multiplication.

MATERIALS

Stephanie shared *P. Bear's New Year's Party* with second and third graders. In both classes, she read the book once, just for the children's enjoyment of it, and then again to introduce the math investigation.

In her first reading to the second graders, she stopped after reading three or four pages and asked the students what they noticed about the animals in the story. Jason raised his hand.

"All the animals are black and white," he said.

"What other animals do you think Mr. Lewis might have put in his book?" Stephanie asked.

"Skunks!" Brent exclaimed.

"Penguins," Larry suggested.

Beth added, "Black bears."

Stephanie asked the class to check these predictions as she read. The children were interested in finding out if their predictions were right. When Stephanie finished the story, Jamie raised her hand. "We were right about the penguins, but we forgot about pandas," she said.

Before Stephanie read the book a second time, she told the children to see what they could notice about the illustrations. "The author put some interesting details in the pictures that I want you to look for," she told them.

When she finished reading, she asked, "What did you notice?"

"All the pictures are black and white," Scott said, "except for the flag on the mailbox and P. Bear's bow tie. They're red."

"It's daytime at the beginning and night at the end," Audrey noticed.

"I know one," Jason said. "The time on the clock is in red and so is the word that says what time it is."

"The number of animals that comes matches the time!" Jane said.

"Wow, there's a lot to notice in this book," Stephanie said. "What do you think about the question at the end? Do you think you could figure out how many guests came to P. Bear's party?"

"Yes!" the class chorused.

Stephanie continued with the directions. "I want you to work in pairs and figure out the total number of guests that came to P. Bear's party," she said. "But I'm interested in more than just your answer. I'm also interested in your thinking about how you solved this problem. You may use anything in the room that will help you. On your paper I want you to tell exactly what you did to solve the problem. You can use numbers, words, pictures, or any combination of these."

The energy in the room was evident as they got started. The children felt confident about solving the problem. Stephanie finds that the more opportunities children have to solve problems, the more comfortable they become approaching them. The students in this class had learned that although they might need a few tries, they were capable of making sense of difficult problems.

Melanie and Jose headed for the bin of Snap Cubes. They made stacks of cubes, arranged them like stairsteps, and counted them.

Brent and Timothy made tally marks to represent the guests. They noticed a pattern in the tallies, that each of their subtotals was a "doubles plus one" fact. Although they thought this was a great discovery, they still needed to resort to counting the tallies to find their answer.

Scott and Jason listed the numbers from *1* to *12* on their paper. They added the numbers in pairs—1 + 2, then 3 + 4, then 5 + 6, and so on—to get subtotals. Then they added the subtotals in pairs and continued this way until they had only two numbers to add. (See Figure 13–1.)

Stephanie noticed Amelia and Larry pointing to the clock on the wall, and she asked them to tell her what they were thinking. Amelia said, "There's a clock in the book, so we're using the clock to add the numbers." When Stephanie walked by them later, they had added tally

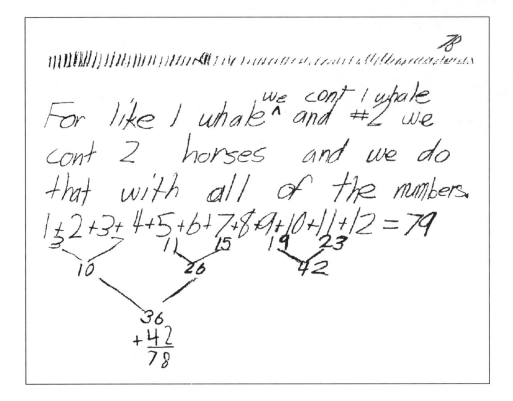

marks to their paper. Larry looked up as she watched them work. "We wanted to be sure," he said.

Emma and Jolie started drawing pictures, but they also switched to tally marks when drawing became tedious. As Stephanie watches children work, one thing she looks for is their willingness to move from one strategy that isn't working to another that might work better. (See Figure 13–2.)

Timothy and Brent raised their hands and called Stephanie over to look at their paper. They explained their solution to her and were ready for a new challenge. She decided to suggest a follow-up problem and give it to the whole class. Stephanie asked the children for their attention and posed another question.

"P. Bear wanted to give out party favors at the end of his party," she said. "Since his party was ending late at night, he decided to give out slippers. How many pairs of slippers will P. Bear need to order?" Stuart's hand shot up.

"What about the killer whale?" he asked. "He doesn't have any feet, so he won't get a party favor." This idea seemed unacceptable, so Stuart suggested that the whale should get one pair of "flipper slippers." Everyone agreed.

Brent and Timothy got to work on this problem, and the others returned to working on the first question. Stephanie listened to Brent and Timothy talk about the slipper question.

"Some of the animals have four feet, but some have two," Timothy said.

First, we tried to draw pictures but that didn't work! Then, we tally marked. We conted by fives. We did it like this. Answer: 79

"Yeah, like geese only need two slippers because they can't wear them on their wings," Brent added.

The boys started to make tally marks for slippers as they retold the story together. However, they soon abandoned this strategy and went to get cubes. They stacked them to represent each page, starting with a stack of two cubes for the whale's flippers. Then they made a stack of eight with four each of two colors. Stephanie asked them about that. "Four red for one horse and four blue for the other one," Brent said. As Stephanie left, they continued to make stacks of cubes, but clearly the method was getting cumbersome for them.

Amelia and Larry also finished the first problem and were interested in the slipper question. As they went through the guest list, they used their fingers to count. They wrote down the name of each animal and the number of slippers it would need. Amelia was frowning as Stephanie walked by. She stopped and watched them work.

"I don't know if we're getting them all," Amelia said. "It's hard to keep up when you count on your fingers."

"But we can't think of another way to do it," Larry added.

"Why don't you look at how other groups are working and see if you get any ideas from them?" Stephanie suggested. When she returned a few minutes later, she saw Larry and Amelia still using their fingers and making tallies on another sheet of paper to check.

When all the groups had finished solving the first problem of finding the number of guests at the party, Stephanie called the class together on the rug for sharing. She asked pairs of children to stand up, share their answers, and explain how they had solved the problem. Presentations like these are valuable because when children are so intent on their own solutions, they don't have the chance to consider other ways to solve a problem.

As the first pair shared, the other children listened and looked back at their papers to see if the answers matched. As children presented their solutions, it was hard at times for others to understand because they were so connected to their own strategies. However, Stephanie still thinks it's very important for children to get in the habit of listening to other ideas.

Stephanie asked questions to help the students compare their approaches. For example, after Brent and Timothy explained how they had solved the problem of the number of guests that P. Bear had invited, she asked them how their solution was like Melanie and Jose's. "Our tallies are like pictures of their stacks of cubes," Brent explained.

"I noticed when I looked at your papers that some of you got seventy-eight and some of you got seventy-nine as a solution," Stephanie said. "Why do you think this happened? Can there be more than one right answer?"

Amelia thought for a moment and raised her hand. "There has to be just one answer. If we counted all the animals at the end of the book, we'd get it."

"Maybe some of us counted wrong," Jason said.

Although the children seemed to be in agreement that there should be just one answer, they weren't particularly interested in knowing whether it was seventy-eight or seventy-nine. Each seemed satisfied that his or her answer was right.

"I'll leave the book up here on the chalk tray for anyone who is interested in thinking more about whether there were seventy-eight or seventy-nine guests," Stephanie said.

When all the groups had had a chance to talk about the first problem, Stephanie moved on to the slipper question. She asked the children who had finished solving the problem to tell the class what they had done. "But don't give your solutions," she said. "I don't want to spoil the problem for the students who haven't had time to think about it yet."

As Stephanie listened to students' explanations, she realized that although the children were interested in the slipper problem, it was difficult for these second graders. The numbers were awfully large for children who didn't have multiplication to use as a tool. She left the problem as an option and suggested to the students that they think about it if they were interested.

A Lesson with Third Graders

When Stephanie read the same book to third graders, the students were just as delighted with the story as the second graders had been. For them, however, the first question of figuring the number of guests that came to the party was not really a problem. It was just an exercise in addition. They were more interested in figuring out how many pairs of slippers P. Bear needed to buy. The children were eager to use their budding multiplication skills to find the number of slippers for each group of animals. They liked the fact that the numbers were large and the problem had several steps. When they shared solutions and how they got them, they were eager to show their own thinking and explain it. (See Figures 13–3 and 13–4.)

Sometimes Stephanie doesn't know if a problem will work with a group of children until she tries it. Sometimes the problem she suggests isn't of interest to them, or it's too easy. Other times, the problem is too complicated or the numbers are too large for them to deal with. Although her goal is to avoid frustrating children, she doesn't mind giving them a problem that causes them to struggle a bit. Even if they can't solve the problem, they always learn something in the attempt. Her challenge as a teacher is to decide when to pull back, move on, or offer support. Watching children, talking to them, and listening to their ideas provide her with the information she needs to make those instructional decisions.

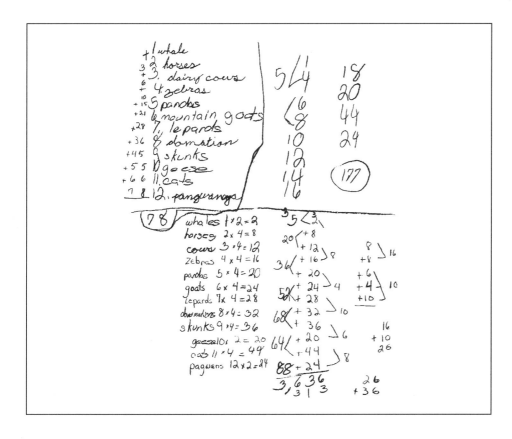

Figure 13–3: Andrea and Katie added to figure out the number of animals and multiplied to determine how many slippers were needed.

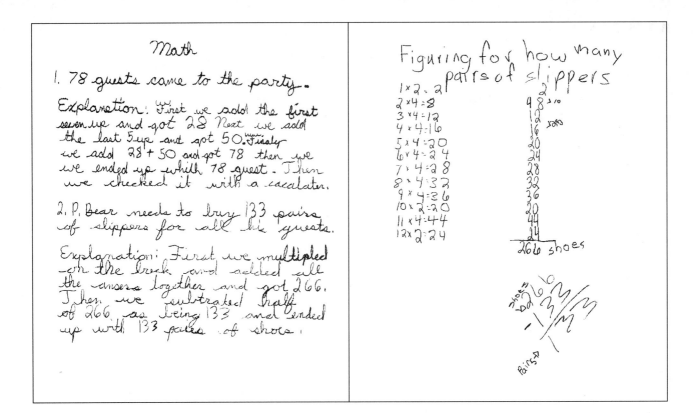

Math

1. 78 guests came to the party.

Explanation: First we add the first seven up and got 28. Next we add the last 5 up and got 50. Finaly we add 28 + 50 and got 78 then we we ended up whith 78 guest. Then we checked it with a cacalater.

2. P. Bear needs to buy 133 pairs of slippers for all his guests.

Explanation: First we multipled on the book and added all the ansers together and got 266. Then we subtrated half of 266 as being 133 and ended up with 133 paies of shoes.

Figuring for how many pairs of slippers

1 × 2 = 2
2 × 4 = 8
3 × 4 = 12
4 × 4 = 16
5 × 4 = 20
6 × 4 = 24
7 × 4 = 28
8 × 4 = 32
9 × 4 = 36
10 × 2 = 20
11 × 4 = 44
12 × 2 = 24

266 shoes

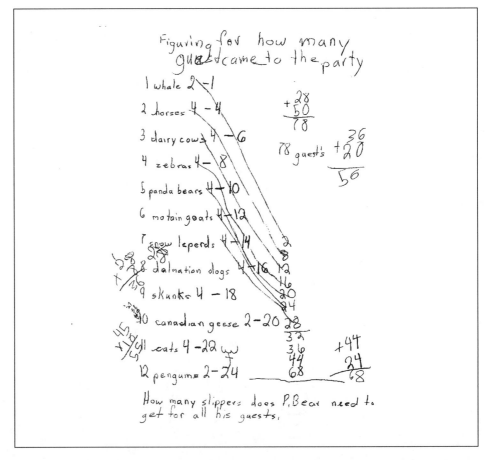

Figuring for how many guest came to the party

1 whale 2 — 1
2 horses 4 — 4
3 dairy cows 4 — 6
4 zebras 4 — 8
5 panda bears 4 — 10
6 motain goats 4 — 12
7 snow leperds 4 — 14
8 dalmation dogs 4 — 16
9 skunks 4 — 18
10 canadian geese 2 — 20
11 cats 4 — 22
12 penguins 2 — 24

+28
50
78

78 guest's +36
20
56

How many slippers does P. Bear need to get for all his guests.

Figure 13–4: Annette and Loren explained their answers carefully and clearly and showed their work.

Pigs Will Be Pigs

*Taught by Stephanie Sheffield
and Rusty Bresser*

Pigs Will Be Pigs: Fun with Math and Money, by Amy Axelrod (1994), is a brightly illustrated tale of the Pig family's search for enough money to feed the whole family. The Pigs begin tearing the house apart looking for loose change and forgotten bills. They put all the money they find in a shoe box and head for their favorite restaurant, the Enchanted Enchilada, where they eat until they are stuffed. Stephanie Sheffield and Rusty Bresser used the story to provide a context for third-grade lessons that focused on the values of coins and bills and provided practice with adding money.

MATERIALS

Stephanie read *Pigs Will Be Pigs* to third graders as they were beginning to work with decimals. It provided a wonderful way to talk about how decimals are used to represent money numerically. As soon as the hunt began in the story, she and the class started keeping track of the total amount of money the Pigs found.

First, Mr. Pig finds his lucky two-dollar bill. Then Mrs. Pig searches in her bedroom and finds two nickels, five pennies, and one quarter.

"Let's see, how much do they have now?" Stephanie asked. "Two nickels is . . . ?"

"Ten cents!" several children responded.

"And five pennies is five cents," Tamara said. "That's fifteen cents," she added.

"Mrs. Pig also found a quarter. How much is that?" Stephanie asked.

"A quarter is twenty-five cents," Marco said, "but I don't know how much that is altogether."

"Let's write all the amounts on the board and add them together," Stephanie suggested. "Carey, why don't you go to the board and be our first recorder. We'll record each amount the Pig family finds. What did they find first?"

Carey said, "Mr. Pig found two dollars," and he wrote *$2.00* on the board.

"Next, Mrs. Pig found two nickels," Stephanie said. Carey wrote *$.50* under $2.00.

"No, that says fifty cents," Esperanza said. Carey erased the $.50 and wrote *$.10*. Carey also wrote *$.05* and *$.25*, neatly lining up the decimal points.

"When we add money, it helps to keep the columns lined up," Stephanie commented. "That way, you keep the coins separate from the dollars."

Carey wrote the four amounts in a column and drew a line underneath. Then, starting with the dollars, he added. He wrote a *2* in the dollars column and then a *3* in the dimes column. Then Carey stopped as he looked ahead to the pennies. Seeing that he had to add five and five, he erased the 3 and wrote a *4* in the dimes column and a zero under the pennies.

$$\begin{array}{r} \$2.00 \\ \$\ .10 \\ \$\ .05 \\ \underline{\$\ .25} \\ \$2.40 \end{array}$$

Stephanie asked Simone to be the next recorder. For the next page the class discussed how much six dimes was and how much two hundred pennies made. Simone said, "That's two dollars and sixty cents." She recorded *$2.60* under the $2.40. They continued in this way, keeping a running total until they had represented all the money.

The children were delighted by the restaurant menu in the book. They spent some time talking about the choices and reading each menu item. Since they lived in Texas, the children were able to describe their favorite Southwest foods. They all agreed that the special sounded delicious.

The class's next task was to figure out how much the family spent on the specials. "That's a hard problem!" Gayle exclaimed. She came up to the board and wrote: *$7.99 + 7.99 + 7.99 + 7.99 =* .

"It would be easier if it was eight dollars," Esperanza said. "That would be like eight times four," she added, and she thought for a minute. "That's thirty-two."

"Would our answer be more or less than thirty-two?" Stephanie asked.

"Less, because the specials only cost seven dollars and ninety-nine cents each," Nolan said.

"Talk to the person next to you about what the price would be for four specials," Stephanie said.

After a few minutes Stephanie called on Janine. "We think it's thirty-one dollars and ninety-six cents," she said.

"Can you explain how you figured that out?" Stephanie asked.

Janine said, "Each special is a penny less than eight dollars, so that's four pennies less than thirty-two dollars."

"Did anyone figure it a different way?" Stephanie asked. Neil raised his hand. "We started at thirty-two dollars and we counted backwards four."

The last page of the book has a question at the top: "How much money did the Pigs find on their hunt?" It goes on to tell how much each member of the Pig family found and pictures the coins and bills. The class checked its total ($33.67) with the total in the book and found the class total was $1.00 off. Going back and checking their addition on the board, the students didn't find any mistakes. Stephanie opened the book and started to go through the pages again. They solved the mystery when they discovered the page showing Mr. Pig with the dollar bill he had in his wallet at the start.

Next, Stephanie asked, "How much money did the Pigs have left from their thirty-four dollars and sixty-seven cents after they paid thirty-one dollars and ninety-six cents for their dinners?" She had students work in pairs to figure out the answer and then share their solutions with the whole class. Some students used the standard subtraction algorithm, and others counted on from $31.96 to $34.67.

Another Lesson with Third Graders

After Rusty Bresser read *Pigs Will Be Pigs* to his third graders, he had the students estimate how much money the Pigs collected. Rusty recorded all of the students' guesses on the board and was surprised at how close some of them were to the correct answer. Greg guessed $34.50, Timothy guessed $34.00, and Janine guessed $30.05.

Rusty read the book a second time and suggested that the students take notes this time so they could figure out later how much money the Pigs had. The children went to their desks, got pencils and paper, and returned to the front of the room. When he finished reading, Rusty directed the students to figure out how much money the Pig family had collected.

Amelia immediately went to get a calculator. "Amelia always tries to use a calculator first," Rusty reported. "Sometimes this is helpful for her, and sometimes it gets her in trouble. This time she got into a mess because she wasn't sure how to use the key with the decimal point. Timothy tried to help her, but she wanted to do it herself. Eventually, Amelia wrote down all the dollar amounts on the left side of her paper and the cents on the right. She added them separately, coming up with thirty-two dollars and two dollars and twenty-seven cents. Then she added these to get a total of thirty-four dollars and twenty-seven cents." (See Figure 14–1.)

Sam lined up all the dollar amounts in a column and added them; then he did the same with the cents. He took the two totals and added them. To prove to himself that he had the right answer, Sam painstakingly drew pictures of all the coins and bills and labeled them carefully. He was totally focused on his work and pleased with his results. His answer was $34.84.

George kept track in a different way. He wrote down the names of the coins and bills, and as Rusty read, George made tally marks next to the coins Rusty mentioned. However, he was not able to use this information to find a total.

Janine divided her paper into four parts. In the top two sections, she kept track of what Mr. and Mrs. Pig found, and next to that, she

Figure 14–1: Amelia wrote all the dollars on the left side of her paper and all the cents on the right, then added the two totals together to get $34.27.

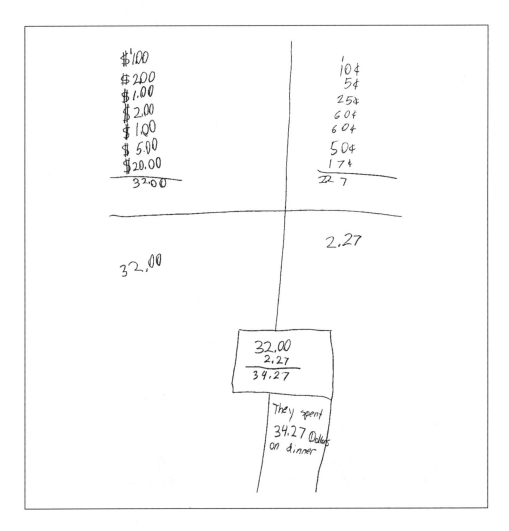

Math and Literature, Grades 2–3

recorded the amounts and added them. In the bottom two sections, she put the money the piglets found and wrote the values of the bills and coins alongside. To add the numbers, she clumped a few amounts together at a time and came up with partial totals. Then she added these together to get her final total. In the end, Janine was only ten cents off.

Amber recorded the amounts first and went back and added the numbers on the side, keeping a running total. Although she had written *$34.00* to start with, she later erased that and recorded her answer as *$40.00*. She wrote: *I added it by putting them together. I think thats the answer.*

After everyone had a chance to work on the problem, Rusty called the class back together. He asked students to share how they had solved the problem, and he recorded all the different amounts they came up with. Then, together, they added the amounts from the book to find the total of $34.67. Makito was pleased that he had gotten the correct answer. (See Figure 14–2.)

For a follow-up lesson, Rusty wrote a shortened version of the menu on chart paper. He wrote the names of the food items (without their descriptions) with the prices alongside. At the children's request, he read the book again. Then he asked the students to look at the menu on the chart paper and decide what the Pig family might have ordered instead of the specials. He suggested that if students wanted to read the complete descriptions of the menu items, they could look in the book.

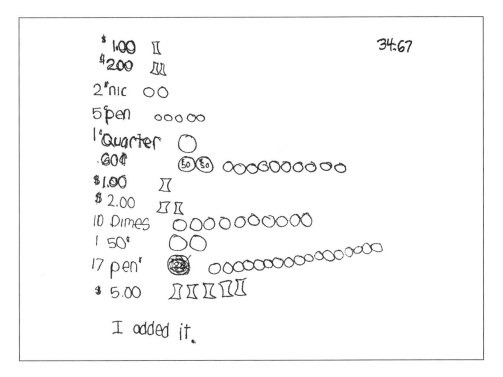

Figure 14–2: Makito wrote and illustrated each amount of money that occurred in the story.

"You need to remember that the Pig family had thirty-four dollars and sixty-seven cents to spend; be sure they don't order more food than they could pay for," Rusty said. "You'll need to write up their order as if you were the waiter or waitress at the Enchanted Enchilada." Rusty talked with the class about what an order form might look like.

"You also need to find out how much change the Pigs would have left over after they paid for their dinner," he added. Rusty reminded the children about using decimals to separate the dollars from the cents. He did this with a light touch, knowing that not all of his students were ready to use this information.

Rusty had students work in pairs because he felt it would strengthen their work and give them the support they needed to do the computations. However, he asked them to record their work individually. As Rusty watched them work, he noticed how animated their discussions were. The children pored over the menu, talking about which foods they liked and which they hadn't ever eaten. (See Figures 14–3 and 14–4.)

Figure 14–3: Sam designed a menu, selected foods for dinner, and listed the total amount spent and the change the Pigs would receive.

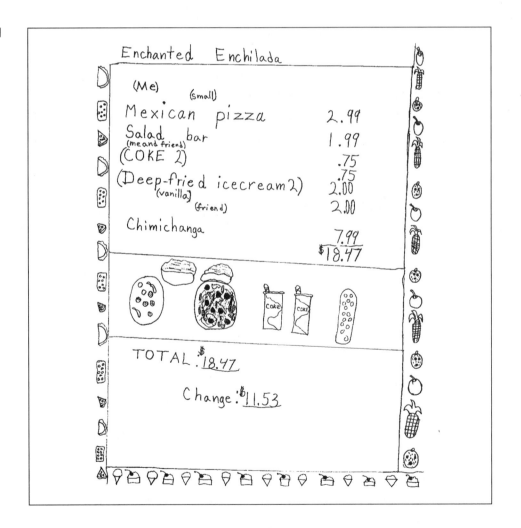

Figure 14–4: Tyler spent
almost the entire $34.67.

Rusty commented later, "They really enjoyed this activity. They liked being able to make choices. This problem is more accessible for students with different degrees of mathematical power. There isn't just one right answer, and allowing them to make choices made them feel they had control over the problem, which helped motivate them to do the math. In a way, they were creating their own mathematical problem."

Six-Dinner Sid

Taught by Rusty Bresser

Six-Dinner Sid is a charming story by Inga Moore (1991) about Sid, an enterprising young cat who lives on Aristotle Street. Sid has convinced six people on the street that each is his owner and therefore goes to six different houses and gets six different dinners every night. Rusty Bresser read the book to third graders and gave them the problem of determining how many dinners Sid eats in one week.

MATERIALS

When Rusty Bresser read *Six-Dinner Sid* to his third graders, although some of the children were familiar with the story, they were excited to hear it again. The story reveals that the neighbors on Aristotle Street don't know one another, so all of them think that the cat they are feeding is theirs. The students laughed at the part when the author points out that Sid has to work hard for his dinners because he has to remember six different names—Scaramouche, Bob, Mischief, Sally, Sooty, and Schwartz—and six different ways to behave. Sid's cover is blown when he develops a nasty cough and is taken to the vet six different times! The vet becomes suspicious, checks his appointment book, finds out that all six black cats live on Aristotle Street, and calls the owners. After that, the neighbors make sure that Sid is fed only one dinner a day. The students enjoyed the twist at the end of the story when Sid moves to another street.

After finishing the book, Rusty posed a problem for the students to solve. He asked, "How many dinners did Sid eat in one week when he lived on Aristotle Street?" The class was in the middle of a unit on multiplication, and Rusty planned to look at how his students would solve this problem to assess whether they understood the concept of multiplication and if they were comfortable using it. When he gave the class the problem, he didn't explain that this was a multiplication problem or suggest that they use multiplication to solve it. All he told the students was, "You can work with a partner, but each of you has to record your own work."

As the students worked, Rusty circulated, listening to the students and looking at their work. He noticed that Scott began by drawing six houses, numbering them *1* to *6*, and writing the numeral *7* in each. Scott explained, "The one to six are the house numbers, and the sevens are there because Sid ate seven meals at each house in one week."

When Rusty looked at Scott's paper later, he saw that Scott had solved the problem by adding seven six times. Also, he had written a multiplication sentence: $7 \times 6 = 42$. Rusty had taught the students that 7×6 means seven groups of six, but that the answer is the same for 7×6 and 6×7, or whenever the factors are reversed. On his paper, however, Scott's sentence didn't match his drawing. (See Figure 15–1.)

Dylan and his partner, Tyrone, drew several pictures on their papers showing seven groups of six and six groups of seven. This showed Rusty that they understood the commutative nature of multiplication. Dylan struggled both with math and with writing. He wrote: *The ansoir is 42 We did 7 × 6 and it = 42 We did it on a cocelate [calculator].*

"Why did you use a calculator?" Rusty asked him. "Can you explain that on your paper?" Dylan wrote: *We yousd a cacelate becaus I cod noln't figr it out and it was to had.*

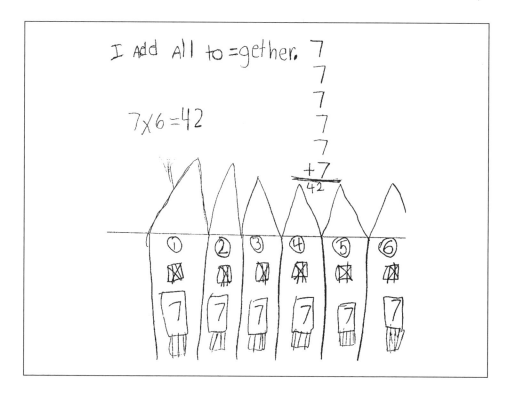

Figure 15–1: Scott added seven six times and drew the houses Sid visited each day.

Dana drew tally marks on her paper, drawing and circling groups of seven tally marks. She drew seven groups. Dana also wrote the number sentence 6 × 7 = 42, not noticing that she had drawn an extra group of seven. Rusty asked her how she figured out that six times seven was forty-two, and Dana answered, "I just know it."

"But why did you draw seven groups of tally marks?" Rusty asked.

Dana counted and said, "Oops, there should only be six."

Amber's drawing showed another way to represent the problem. She drew seven boxes, labeling them for each day of the week, and indicated in each box that Sid ate six dinners. She also wrote a multiplication sentence: 6 × 7 = 42. In this instance, Amber's sentence should have been 7 × 6 = 42, which is a way to represent seven groups with six in each. (See Figure 15–2.)

Jeremy first started to draw pictures to solve the problem. When this didn't seem to work for him, he moved to counting as a strategy. He was not comfortable counting by sixes, but he knew he could count by fives. He told Rusty, "I couldn't count by sixes so I counted by fives seven times. That works if Sid ate five dinners each night. So then I added on seven more to make forty-two."

"Jeremy always tries to let me know how he's making sense of what he's doing," Rusty said.

Figure 15–2: Amber explained her thinking and illustrated Sid's dinners for each day of the week.

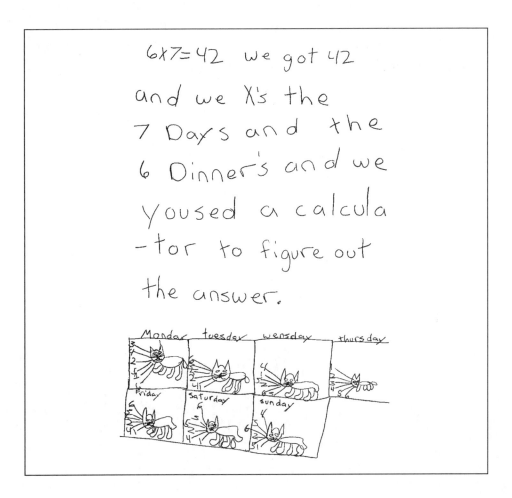

Math and Literature, Grades 2–3

As a follow-up to this problem-solving assignment, Rusty led a class discussion, focusing on the difference in interpretations when factors are reversed. He drew two different pictures on the board to represent the problem. One was similar to what Scott and others had drawn—six houses with the numeral 7 in each to represent the number of meals eaten in each house in one week. The other was similar to what Amber and others had drawn—seven boxes, labeled for the days of the week, with the numeral 6 inside each to represent the number of meals eaten each day of the week.

Rusty referred to the game of *Circles and Stars* that the students had learned at the beginning of the unit on multiplication. (See *Teaching Arithmetic: Lessons for Introducing Multiplication, Grade 3* [Burns 2001].) To play that game, students roll a die twice. The first number tells how many circles to draw and the second number tells how many stars to draw in each circle. For example, if a student first rolled a 6 and then a 2, he would draw six circles with two stars in each. The students knew to write 6 × 2 to represent the six groups of two. If he first rolled a 2 and then a 6, however, he would draw two circles with six stars in each and write 2 × 6. The students knew, however, that the total number of stars was the same in both cases.

Rusty related the game to the two different drawings to help the students see that in the drawing of the houses, there were six groups (the houses) with seven in each (the meals Sid ate in each house). The other drawing showed seven groups (the days of the week) with six in each (the meals Sid ate on each day). While the two different representations both produce the same answer, Rusty still wanted the children to think about how to use multiplication to interpret situations.

See Figures 15–3 through 15–5 for other students' solutions.

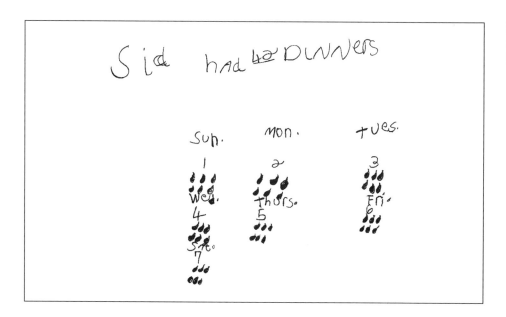

Figure 15–3: Kimberly made groups of popcorn kernels to find the answer.

Figure 15–4: Russell made a group of six for each day of the week. However, he miscounted, and his answer was off by one.

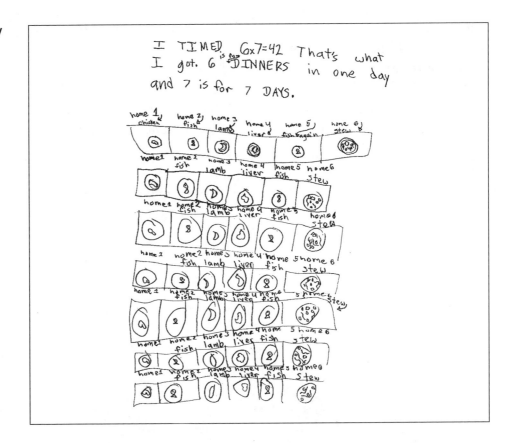

Figure 15–5: Seth carefully drew the menu for each dinner to illustrate his answer.

Stay in Line

Taught by Leyani von Rotz

In Teddy Slater's *Stay in Line* (1996), twelve girls and boys set off on a field trip to the zoo. By showing how the children line up two by two, sit on the bus three by three, crowd into two rows to look at the chicks, and so on, the book helps children see how a dozen children can be grouped in different ways. After reading the book to a class of second graders, Leyani von Rotz engaged the children in recording different ways to break the number twelve into smaller groups.

MATERIALS

Leyani gathered the second graders on the rug and showed them the cover of *Stay in Line*. Several of the children read the title aloud.

"What do you think this book might be about?" Leyani asked the class.

"Maybe it's about lining up like when we go to lunch," Samantha said.

"The teacher wants them to stay in line," Jasmine added.

"Well, let's see," Leyani said and read the story aloud. She began, "Twelve girls and boys set off for the zoo. Six pairs of children lined up, two by two." For this first reading, Leyani didn't stop for discussion but read the story straight through. The book shows the children marching down the school steps in three rows of four, climbing onto the bus and sitting in four rows of three to a seat, entering the zoo in one line of four and one line of eight, walking single file to the henhouse, crowding into two rows of six to look at the chicks, standing in one row of twelve to see the llamas, playing with the bunnies in twos and threes, and finally taking a nap in one heap of the twelve of them.

Leyani then reread the book, this time stopping to discuss each page. For the page that shows six pairs of children lined up two by two, Leyani said, "Let's count the children by twos and see if all twelve of them are in the picture." As Leyani pointed to each pair of children, the children counted along with her, "Two, four, six, eight, ten, twelve."

"What number sentence could we write that goes with this page?" Leyani asked.

Ibraheem responded, "Two plus two plus two, like that." Leyani recorded on the board:

$$2 + 2 + 2$$

"What else should I write?" she asked.

"You have to keep going," Ibraheem said.

"Tell me what to write next," Leyani said.

"You have to go plus two plus two plus two," he responded. Leyani added on to what she had written.

$$2 + 2 + 2 + 2 + 2 + 2$$

"That's it," Ibraheem said.

"Can you finish the sentence with an equals sign?" Leyani asked.

"Oh yeah," Ibraheem said. "You write equals and then twelve." Leyani added this to what she had already recorded:

$$2 + 2 + 2 + 2 + 2 + 2 = 12$$

Taking the time with Ibraheem to give a complete number sentence was valuable for providing a model for the other children about what she expected. "Does anyone have another idea for a number sentence we could write for this page?" Leyani asked.

Alan said, "You could write eleven plus one equals twelve." Leyani wasn't sure how Alan's idea connected to the page, but she wanted to acknowledge Alan's mathematical thinking. So she recorded it on the board:

$$11 + 1 = 12$$

"How does this sentence show what is happening on the page?" Leyani then asked.

Leyani was surprised by Alan's answer. He said, "See that girl getting her hair pulled? She's the one in my sentence."

"Plus the teacher makes thirteen," Annie piped up, including the teacher also pictured on the page.

Leyani was only thinking about different combinations for twelve, but she followed up Annie's idea. "What number sentence should I write?" Leyani asked.

"Twelve plus one equals thirteen," Annie said. Leyani recorded:

$$12 + 1 = 13$$

"Any other ideas?" Leyani asked.

"You could do six plus six," Purna said and then added, after Leyani recorded and looked at her, "equals twelve." Leyani completed the sentence:

$$6 + 6 = 12$$

"And tell us how this sentence goes with the page," Leyani said.

"There are six and six," Purna said, coming up and showing with her finger first the six children on the left and then the six on the right.

"Any other ideas?" Leyani asked. No one had an idea, so Leyani offered one. She wasn't planning on introducing the children to multiplication at this time, but she took the opportunity to present the notation. "I see six groups of two, the way Ibraheem did, but I have another way to write the number sentence—six groups of two equals twelve," Leyani said, recording on the board and writing a multiplication sign when she said "groups of."

$$6 \times 2 = 12$$

Leyani then turned the page to show the children marching out the school door and down the steps in three rows of four. Again, she asked the children to give her number sentences, recording their ideas and having them explain how the sentences showed what was happening on the page.

"Who knows what a dozen is?" Leyani asked, writing *dozen* on the board. Some children knew that there were twelve in a dozen, but for others this was new information. For the rest of the lesson, Leyani used the word *dozen* often to help the children become familiar with it.

Leyani continued in this way for the rest of the book. She asked the students to focus just on the children in the book and not to worry about including the teacher. She was pleased with the variation in the children's ideas. For example, for the page that shows the children lined up in single file to go to the henhouse, Jacob suggested $1 + 1 + 1 + 1 + 1 + 1 + 1 + 1 + 1 + 1 + 1 + 1 = 12$. Then Tomo suggested $4 + 8 = 12$ and explained, "Four of the children have hats."

But Darnell had a different way to interpret the hats. "Two of the hats are falling off their heads," he said and suggested $2 + 2 + 8 = 12$.

Then Samantha suggested $12 + 0 = 12$. "They're all together," she explained.

Leyani then asked the students to think of all the ways that a dozen children could line up. "I'd like you to record your ideas on paper with number sentences and also with pictures," she said. "But it will take too long to draw children. What ideas do you have about what you could draw easily to represent the children?" The students made several suggestions, including footballs, hearts, triangles, circles, squares, ovals, and lines. Leyani sent the children back to their tables and they got to work. (See Figures 16–1 through 16–4.)

Figure 16–1: Ally used hearts to represent the children.

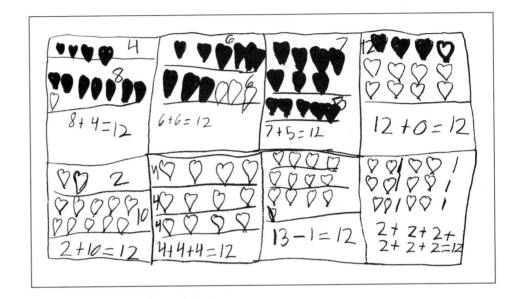

Figure 16–2: Sam, a student who struggled, was able to write and illustrate only one number sentence.

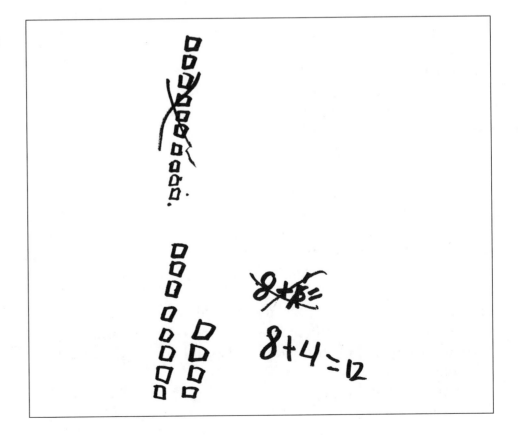

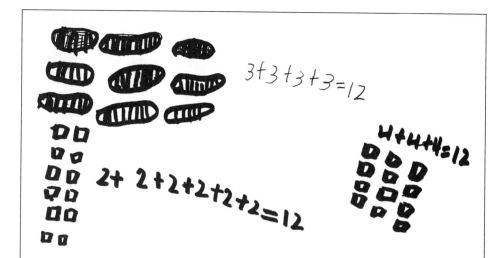

Figure 16–3: Jagjit wrote number sentences with repeating addends.

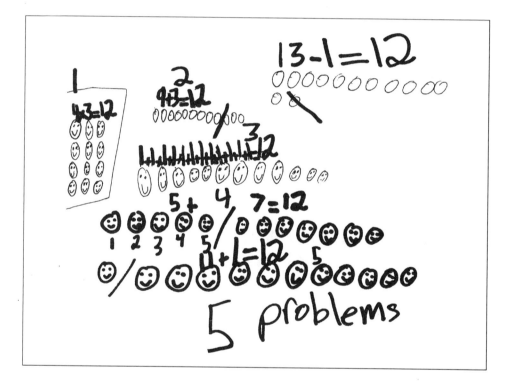

Figure 16–4: Jameel wrote six sentences, using multiplication for one of them, subtraction for another, and addition for the rest.

Ten Friends

Taught by Marilyn Burns

Bruce Goldstone's book *Ten Friends* (2001) uses rhymes and bright illustrations to suggest different ways to invite ten friends to tea; for example, eight trusty tailors with two proud plumbers or seven salty sailors with three loud drummers. Ten combinations of ten guests are suggested in all, including some with three, four, and more groups of guests. At the back of the book, the author lists all of the ways to represent ten using two addends, three addends, and so on up to ten addends. Marilyn Burns read the story to a class of second graders and then gave the students the challenge of writing as many different number sentences as they could that showed different combinations of numbers that add to ten.

MATERIALS

color tiles or other counters, 10 per student

Marilyn gathered the second graders on the rug and showed them *Ten Friends*. Some of the children commented on the characters shown on the cover.

"The fireman has a two on his hat," Harry noticed.

"The fireman is a crocodile!" Charlie commented.

Cara had been quietly counting and then announced, "There are ten friends on the cover." Together the students counted the characters as Marilyn named and pointed to them—a fireman, a frog, a lobster, an elephant, a mouse, a baby chick, a cat, a rooster, a sheep, and an octopus.

Marilyn opened the book and read the first page aloud, which asks the reader to name the ten friends he or she would invite to tea. Several children immediately raised their hands, interested in telling the class who they would invite to tea. However, Marilyn signaled them to lower their hands and turned the page to continue reading the book.

She showed them the next spread with the first possibility—inviting ten firefighters. Then she turned to the next spread, which shows nine grizzly bears and one friendly forest ranger. The next spread suggests eight tailors and two plumbers.

Before turning the page again, Marilyn said, "So the first idea was to invite ten firefighters, the second idea was to invite nine bears and one forest ranger, and the third idea was to invite eight tailors and two plumbers. What numbers do you think will be on the next page?" Some children quickly predicted that seven and three would be on the next page; others guessed other numbers; some didn't guess at all. Marilyn turned the page to reveal that invited to tea were seven sailors and three drummers.

"Look," Celia said, "the sailors are lobsters!"

"And the drummers are octopuses," Cole added.

"I know what comes next," Hannah said.

"Raise your hand if you think you know what numbers are on the next page," Marilyn said. After most of the children raised their hands, she added, "Whisper your idea to your neighbor." Then she turned the page to reveal six ballerinas and four frogs.

"And what numbers will come next?" Marilyn asked. "Let's say it together in a whisper voice."

"Five and five," the children said in unison. Marilyn turned the page to show five shepherds and five sheep.

Children who wanted to predict the numbers on the next page waved their hands in the air. However, because the book now shifted to using more than two addends to show ten friends, Marilyn didn't call on anyone. "The next page is very different," she said. She turned the page and read, "Would you invite four scuba divers, three chauffeurs, and three bus drivers?"

"Hey, that's weird," Travis said.

"It still works," Manuel said. "It still makes ten."

"Are you all sure about that?" Marilyn asked.

"You can count them," Elena suggested. As Marilyn pointed to the characters shown, the children counted to ten.

"How could we be sure without counting?" she asked. "How can we add up four and three and three?"

Cara said, "Four and three is seven, and three more is ten."

Marilyn then said, turning the page, "Let's see what combination of ten friends comes next." Shown on the next spread are one quilter, two sweater knitters, three giggly babies, and four baby-sitters. "Do these numbers add up to ten?" she asked. "Talk with your neighbor about this."

After a few moments, Marilyn called the class to attention. All agreed that the numbers added to ten. Dan explained, "One plus two is three, and three plus three is six, and six plus four is ten."

"Let's see who gets invited on the next page," Marilyn said. The next spread shows two each of teachers, trolls, tycoons, ventriloquists, and baboons.

"Who knows what a ventriloquist is?" she asked.

"Is it a puppet?" Travis guessed.

"That's close," Marilyn responded. "A ventriloquist works with a puppet and talks for it, but the ventriloquist tries not to move his or her lips so you think the puppet is really talking."

"It's ten," Cara said, shifting the conversation back to the numbers. "It's easy. You just count two, four, six, eight, ten."

The next spread shows the last configuration of guests—one prince, one painter, two potters, one diner, one miner, one major, and three otters. Again, the students verified that the six numbers added to ten. The book continues for a few more spreads, reviewing the characters presented in the book and asking how many there would be if all of them showed up. The last illustration in the book shows a 10-by-10 grid with all of the characters pictured.

Marilyn then introduced the assignment that the students were going to do. "The book showed ten different combinations of guests to invite if you were inviting ten friends to tea," she said. "One of the suggestions was to invite nine bears and one forest ranger. Watch as I write a number sentence that describes this." Marilyn turned to the board and wrote:

$$9 + 1 = 10$$

She then said, "Another suggestion was to ask eight tailors and two plumbers." She wrote another number sentence on the board:

$$8 + 2 = 10$$

"Another suggestion was for five shepherds and five sheep," Marilyn said. "What would I write for that?"

"Five plus five," Cara volunteered. Marilyn recorded:

$$5 + 5$$

"And what do I write to show that this would be ten friends?" Marilyn asked.

"Oh," Cara said, "equals ten." Marilyn completed the number sentence.

$$5 + 5 = 10$$

Marilyn then asked, "What number sentence would I write for one quilter, two knitters, three babies, and four baby-sitters?" She called on Charlie and recorded as he reported:

$$1 + 2 + 3 + 4 = 10$$

"That's cool how the numbers go in order," Travis commented.

Marilyn then explained to the students what they were to do. "These are four number sentences with numbers that add to ten. Your job is to try to write as many different number sentences as you can that show ways to add numbers to equal ten."

"Can we do subtraction?" Dan wanted to know.

"That's a good idea, but not today," Marilyn responded. "I'm interested in how many different combinations of numbers you can think of that add to ten."

"Can we use negative numbers?" Manuel asked. He had recently discovered negative numbers and was fascinated by them.

"For today, let's not use any negative numbers," Marilyn said.

No other student had a question. Marilyn made two last comments. "Each of your number sentences should use different numbers. For example, if you include the first sentence that I wrote—nine plus one equals ten—then you shouldn't also write a sentence with the same numbers, like this." She wrote on the board: *1 + 9 = 10.* "You don't need to write this sentence. It uses the same numbers, just in a different order."

Marilyn made one more suggestion before the students got to work. She took ten tiles and placed them, equally spaced, in a line on the rug so that all of the children could see them. She moved the two tiles at the right end away so the tiles were now in two groups—eight and two.

"Which number sentence on the board do you think matches the way I've arranged the tiles?" she asked. It was obvious to the children that the sentence was $8 + 2 = 10$. Marilyn then rearranged the tiles into four groups of one, two, three, and four tiles.

"Which number sentence on the board does this arrangement match?" she asked. Again, it was obvious to the children that the matching sentence was $1 + 2 + 3 + 4 = 10$.

"The tiles can help me think of other sentences I haven't written yet," she said, rearranging them into three groups of three, four, and three.

"What number sentence could I write for this arrangement?" Marilyn asked. She called on Celia.

"Three plus four plus three," she said.

"Equals ten," Cara added. "You have to write equals ten, too."

"Oh yeah," Celia said. Marilyn recorded the number sentence on the board: *3 + 4 + 3 = 10.*

She then had the children return to their seats and begin working. As they went to their tables, she walked around the room and distributed ten tiles to each of them. "Do we have to use them?" Manuel asked.

"No," she responded. "But I'll just leave them here in case you decide that they would be helpful."

The children approached the problem in different ways. Cara first wrote sentences with two addends, then wrote sentences with three addends, and then sentences with four addends. (See Figure 17–1.) This wasn't a typical approach—most of the children wrote sentences randomly. Some of the students used the tiles, making and recording different arrangements; some children didn't use the tiles at first but resorted to them after they ran out of ideas; some children chose to

Figure 17–1: Cara approached the problem in an organized manner.

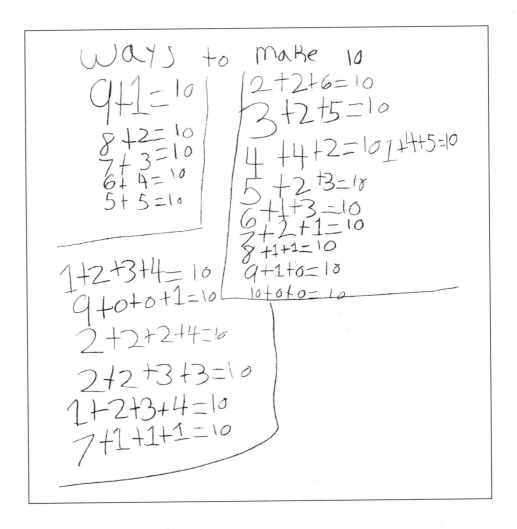

Math and Literature, Grades 2–3

work without referring to the tiles at all. (See Figures 17–2 and 17–3.) Travis and Manuel were eager to find all of the possible combinations, but most of the children had had enough after filling a page. (See Figure 17–4.)

A colleague watching the lesson asked Marilyn why she hadn't shown the children the last page in the book, where the author organizes all of the addition sentences according to the number of addends. Marilyn responded that she had chosen not to show the page because she didn't want to overwhelm the students. "But it's possible that the structure would have encouraged more of the children to look for all of the sentences," she added. However, the colleague's comment sparked an idea. The next day, Marilyn posted a piece of chart paper

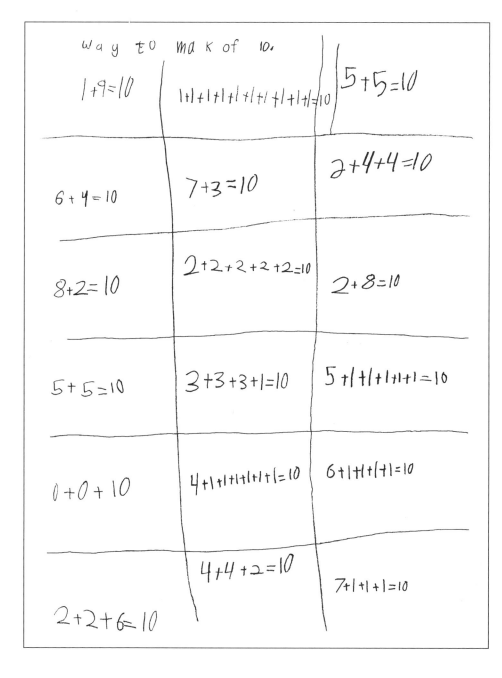

Figure 17–2: Celia drew boxes and wrote a number sentence in each, working with the tiles to find different combinations.

Figure 17–3: Dan showed Marilyn the pattern of the first addends in each of his groups of number sentences.

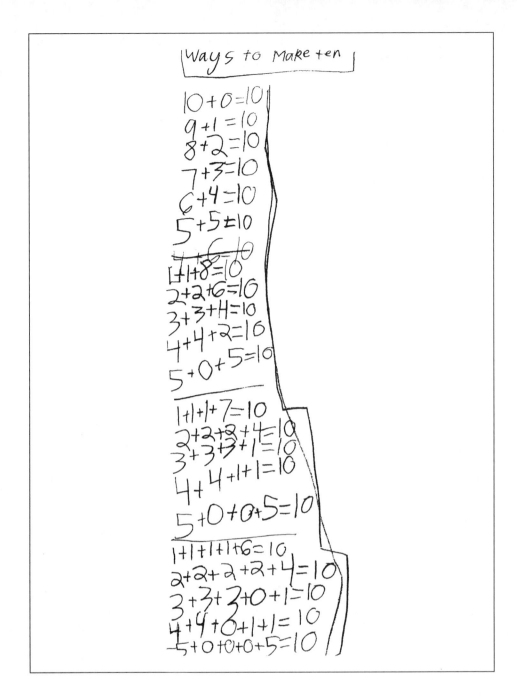

Ways to Make ten

$$10 + 0 = 10$$
$$9 + 1 = 10$$
$$8 + 2 = 10$$
$$7 + 3 = 10$$
$$6 + 4 = 10$$
$$5 + 5 = 10$$

$$1 + 1 + 8 = 10$$
$$2 + 2 + 6 = 10$$
$$3 + 3 + 4 = 10$$
$$4 + 4 + 2 = 10$$
$$5 + 0 + 5 = 10$$

$$1 + 1 + 1 + 7 = 10$$
$$2 + 2 + 2 + 4 = 10$$
$$3 + 3 + 3 + 1 = 10$$
$$4 + 4 + 1 + 1 = 10$$
$$5 + 0 + 0 + 5 = 10$$

$$1 + 1 + 1 + 1 + 6 = 10$$
$$2 + 2 + 2 + 2 + 4 = 10$$
$$3 + 3 + 3 + 0 + 1 = 10$$
$$4 + 4 + 0 + 1 + 1 = 10$$
$$5 + 0 + 0 + 0 + 5 = 10$$

ruled into nine sections and labeled them for the numbers of addends from two to ten. She purposely gave less space to the bottom sections because she knew that they would have fewer entries.

She went around the room, asking each child to read a sentence from his or her paper that she could record on the chart. "Find a number sentence on your paper that I haven't written up yet," she instructed. After about thirty number sentences were on the chart, Marilyn stopped the activity and said, "If you think of another sentence that we don't have up here, write it down and show it to me. Then we can add it to our chart." The students continued filling in the chart whenever they thought of a new sentence to add.

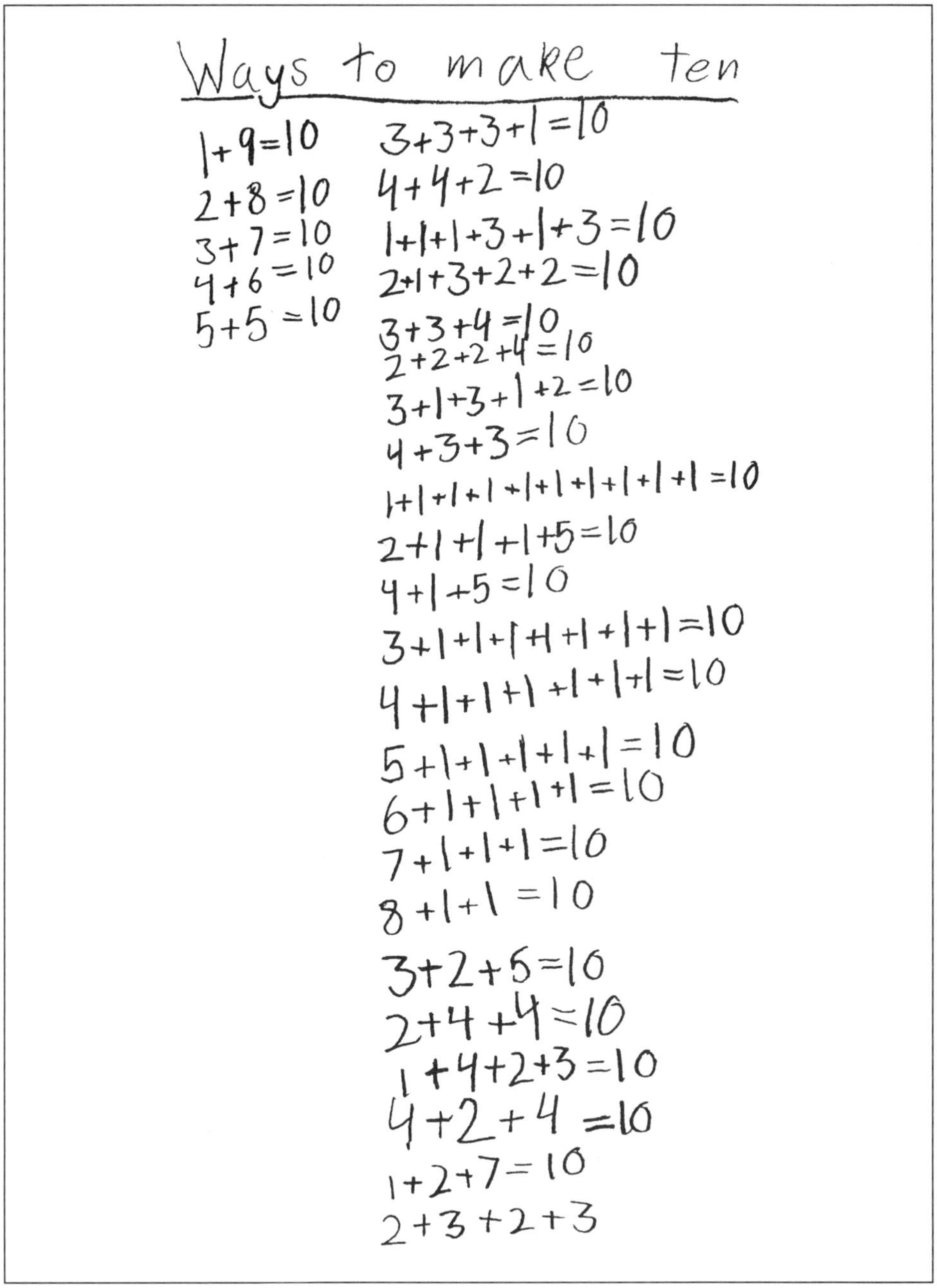

Ways to make ten

$1 + 9 = 10$	$3 + 3 + 3 + 1 = 10$
$2 + 8 = 10$	$4 + 4 + 2 = 10$
$3 + 7 = 10$	$1 + 1 + 1 + 3 + 1 + 3 = 10$
$4 + 6 = 10$	$2 + 1 + 3 + 2 + 2 = 10$
$5 + 5 = 10$	$3 + 3 + 4 = 10$
	$2 + 2 + 2 + 4 = 10$
	$3 + 1 + 3 + 1 + 2 = 10$
	$4 + 3 + 3 = 10$
	$1 + 1 + 1 + 1 + 1 + 1 + 1 + 1 + 1 + 1 = 10$
	$2 + 1 + 1 + 1 + 5 = 10$
	$4 + 1 + 5 = 10$
	$3 + 1 + 1 + 1 + 1 + 1 + 1 + 1 = 10$
	$4 + 1 + 1 + 1 + 1 + 1 + 1 = 10$
	$5 + 1 + 1 + 1 + 1 + 1 = 10$
	$6 + 1 + 1 + 1 + 1 = 10$
	$7 + 1 + 1 + 1 = 10$
	$8 + 1 + 1 = 10$
	$3 + 2 + 5 = 10$
	$2 + 4 + 4 = 10$
	$1 + 4 + 2 + 3 = 10$
	$4 + 2 + 4 = 10$
	$1 + 2 + 7 = 10$
	$2 + 3 + 2 + 3$

Figure 17–4: At the end of class, Travis told Marilyn proudly that he had written twenty-eight sentences.

A Three Hat Day

Taught by Marilyn Burns

Laura Geringer's book *A Three Hat Day* (1985) is ideal to read to young children. Delightfully illustrated by Arnold Lobel, the book tells the story of R.R. Pottle the Third, a man who truly loves hats and has a wonderful collection but is also unhappy because he is lonely. However, his hats become the way to his happiness. Marilyn Burns read the book to a class of third graders and engaged the children in a problem-solving lesson.

MATERIALS

Marilyn gathered the third graders on the rug so that they could more easily see the illustrations in *A Three Hat Day*. She showed them the cover and asked what they noticed.

"I like his sailor hat," Sarah said.

"Hey, he's wearing a bunch of hats," Leif noticed.

"There are three of them," Julia added. "See, that's what the title says."

"But what kind of hat is tied around his chin?" Daniel wanted to know.

"See if you can figure that out as I read the story," Marilyn said and began reading. The second page in the book describes many of R.R. Pottle's hats, and the illustration on the facing page shows a dozen different pictures of R.R. Pottle wearing a different hat in each.

After examining the illustration, Daniel said, "I get it. The one tied around his chin is a bathing cap." The others agreed.

Marilyn continued the story, revealing that R.R. Pottle came from a family of collectors. His father collected canes and his mother liked umbrellas, and together they liked to go for long walks in the rain. After his parents died, R.R. Pottle lived alone and, at times, he was very lonely. One day, to cheer himself up, he put on the three hats shown in the cover illustration—a bathing cap, a fireman's helmet, and a sailor hat—and went out for a walk.

On his walk, R.R. happened upon a hat store and made the acquaintance of the woman who owned it. Their common interest in hats drew them together. They fell in love and got married. (And, later, they had a child, R.R. Pottle the Fourth, who, it turns out, didn't like hats, umbrellas, or canes. She loved shoes.)

After reading the story, Marilyn again showed the students the cover of the book. She asked, "Which hat did R.R. Pottle put on first?" After most of the children had raised their hands, Marilyn had them answer together in a whisper voice. "A bathing cap," they said. She repeated this for the other two hats.

Marilyn then presented a problem for the children to solve. "Suppose R.R. Pottle wanted to cheer himself up on another day and put on the same three hats before going for his walk," Marilyn said. "But suppose that he decided to put on the hats in a different order. And then the next day he put the same three hats on in a different order again. The problem for you to solve is to figure out how many days R.R. Pottle could wear those same three hats if each day he put them on in a different order."

"Can he wear other hats, too?" Lisa asked.

Marilyn answered, "For this problem, he wears just these three hats—the bathing cap, the fireman's helmet, and the sailor hat." Marilyn planned to have children who finished early tackle the problem of finding all the ways he could order four hats, but she chose to wait and pose it for students as they completed work on the first problem.

Marilyn then talked to the children about how they were to work. She said, "First think about what can help you solve the problem and how you can organize your paper. Remember to include an explanation about how you solved the problem." Marilyn then wrote on the chalkboard the names of the hats.

bathing cap
fireman's helmet
sailor hat

"Can we draw pictures?" David asked.

"That would be fine if it helps you think and helps you present what you find out," Marilyn responded.

"Can we use abbreviations for the hats?" Melina asked.

"That would be fine," Marilyn answered.

No other students had questions and they all got to work. When children search for all of the ways to order a particular set of items, they are finding the *permutations* of the items. While studying permutations typically doesn't occur until later when students are introduced formerly to ideas about probability, this problem gives students informal experience with the idea. Marilyn didn't introduce the terminology of permutation at this time.

The problem seemed to be accessible for all of the students—they understood the context and the task. Several of the children began by drawing hats, but all dropped this scheme and began to use abbreviations. Their abbreviations, however, differed. Some used A, B, and C; others used B, F, and S; Andy used BC, FC, and SC; Melina used B.H., F.H., and S.H. (See Figures 18–1 through 18–7 for several students' solutions.)

Figure 18–1: Laura and Sammy used drawings to represent their solution.

Figure 18–2: Kimberly and Joanna started by drawing hats and then switched to symbols.

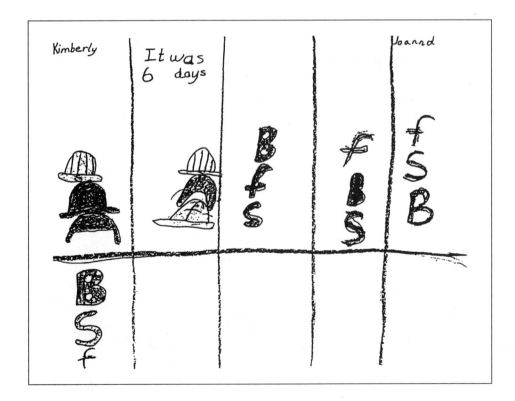

Math and Literature, Grades 2–3

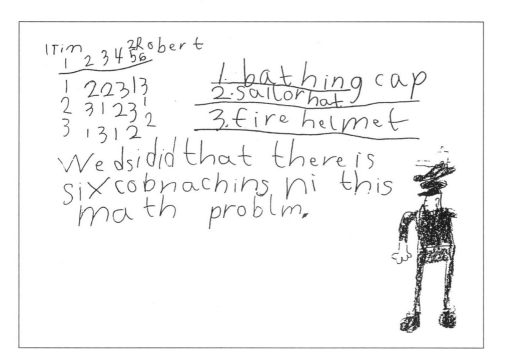

Figure 18–3: Robert and Tim defined their numerical code for the hats.

Figure 18–4: Thayer and Ashleigh drew portraits of R.R. Pottle, each with a different arrangement of hats.

Figure 18–5: Jenee wrote two solutions for each hat on the top and two for each hat on the bottom. Then she eliminated duplicates.

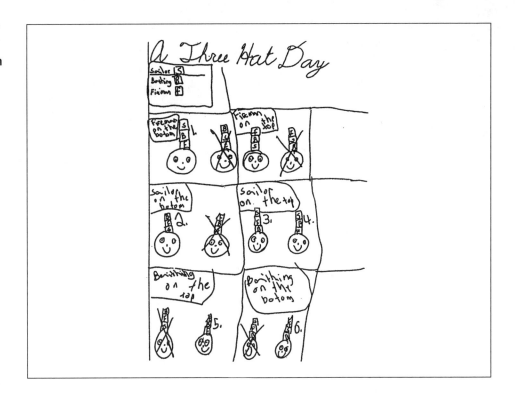

Figure 18–6: Rebecca used trial and error to find the six arrangements.

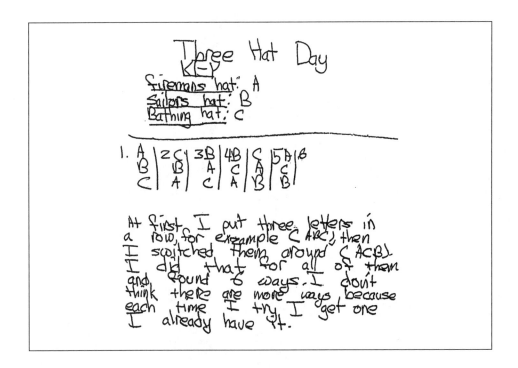

As students completed their solutions, Marilyn gave them the challenge of figuring out how many different ways R.R. Pottle could wear four hats. "Use a top hat for his fourth hat," Marilyn told them. Half of the nineteen children who had time to try this challenge solved it correctly. On their own, two children extended the problem to five hats, making their own choice for the fifth hat.

Math and Literature, Grades 2–3

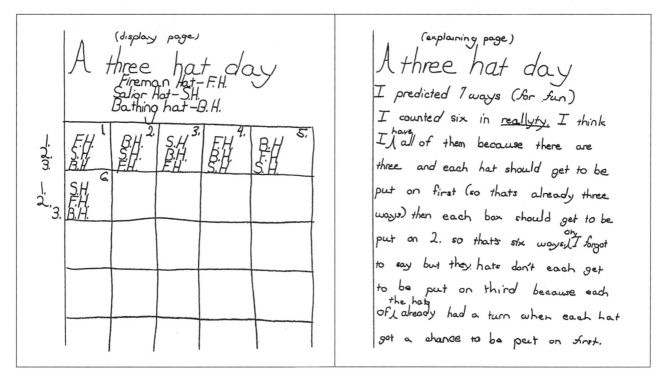

Figure 18–7: Melina's display page showed that she had anticipated more solutions. Her explanation revealed that she had figured out why there were only six arrangements.

A Class Discussion

When Marilyn read the students' papers after class, she noticed that children used different approaches to find all the permutations of hats. She decided to have a follow-up discussion so that the children could see the different ways they had reasoned. Such a discussion would support the important idea that problems can be solved in many different ways.

Marilyn focused on the children's work for the three-hat problem and looked for papers that had two kinds of differences—in the symbols the children used to represent the hats and in the systems they used to be sure they had found all the possible arrangements. She chose seven children's papers and, using a separate large sheet of paper for each, wrote the first three arrangements from each student's solution.

Marilyn again gathered the students on the rug and began by showing them what she had copied from Sam's paper. Sam had used the letter A for the fireman's helmet, B for the shower cap, and C for the sailor hat. He had listed each order vertically.

$$
\begin{array}{ccc}
A & A & B \\
B & C & C \\
C & B & A \\
\end{array}
$$

"What do you think Sam wrote next?" Marilyn asked the class.

About half the children raised their hands. Marilyn called on Brian. "It would be B A C," he said, and then explained, "because he started with A two times and then switched to B." Marilyn confirmed that this was just what Sam had done and added this permutation to the list.

$$
\begin{array}{cccc}
A & A & B & B \\
B & C & C & A \\
C & B & A & C \\
\end{array}
$$

"What do you think Sam wrote next?" she asked. All the children knew that he started with C, but there was disagreement as to whether he had written C B A or C A B. Marilyn acknowledged that both suggestions were possible. "Sometimes we don't have enough information to predict positively what comes next," she said. She told them what Sam had written next, and the others then knew his last entry.

Marilyn then said, "So Sam found six ways that R.R. Pottle could wear his hats."

"Me, too," several others added.

"Yes, you all eventually figured out that R.R. Pottle could wear his hats in six different arrangements. In mathematics, there's a special word that we use to describe arrangements of things, like hats, in different orders. Each arrangement is called a permutation. So there were six permutations of the three hats." Marilyn wrote *permutation* on the board and had the children say the word. Introducing vocabulary in the context of an activity is ideal for helping children learn new math vocabulary.

Marilyn continued the discussion with other children's work. Andy, for example, had used a rotating system. His first three permutations, listed horizontally were as follows:

$$
\begin{array}{ccc}
BC & SC & FC \\
FC & BC & SC \\
SC & FC & BC \\
\end{array}
$$

Marilyn also showed two solutions with randomly ordered arrangements. She wanted to give children the chance to see how using patterns to organize work can make it easier to predict beyond the information that is available. At the same time, however, she didn't want to criticize the work of children who had searched randomly. "There are many different ways to solve problems," she said.

To end the discussion, Marilyn told the class that some of the students had worked on the problem of figuring out how many ways R.R. Pottle could wear four hats. She didn't present their solutions but rather left the problem for students to work on if they wanted to. (See Figures 18–8 and 18–9.)

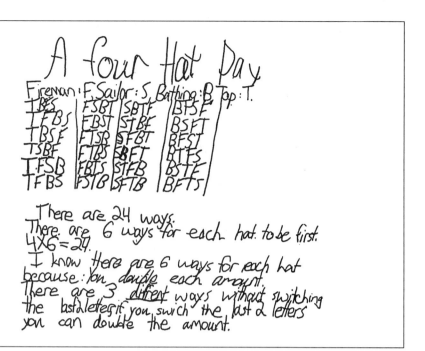

Figure 18–8: Lisa found all twenty-four ways and explained her method.

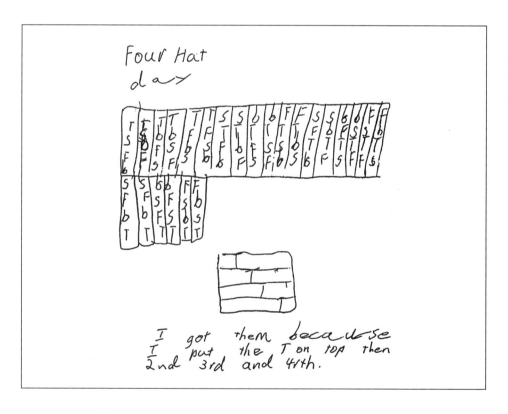

Figure 18–9: Leif repeated the same six arrangements for three hats and inserted the new hat in four different positions.

Two of Everything

Taught by Marilyn Burns

Two of Everything, by Lily Toy Hong (1993), is a Chinese folktale about an elderly couple who find magic right in their own backyard. Mr. Haktak discovers an ancient brass pot in his garden and decides to bring it to the house. He throws his coin purse into the pot for safekeeping. When Mrs. Haktak accidentally drops her hairpin in the pot and reaches in to get it, she pulls out two hairpins and two coin purses! Mr. and Mrs. Haktak realize their good fortune and get to work doubling their valuables. Marilyn Burns read the book to a class of second graders and used the story to engage the students in exploring doubles.

MATERIALS

Marilyn Burns gathered the class of second graders on the rug to read *Two of Everything* aloud to them. The children loved the story. After Mr. Haktak found out that his purse with five gold coins had become two purses with ten gold coins, the children weren't sure what was going to happen next. But they soon caught on about the pot doubling whatever was put into it.

When Mrs. Haktak tripped and fell into the pot, some of the children gasped, horrified, while others broke into giggles. When Mrs. Haktak demanded that Mr. Haktak put the new Mrs. Haktak back into the pot, many of the children protested out loud. After listening to the story, several children had comments.

"That would be a really great pot to have," David said.

"It would help my marble collection," Danny added.

"I liked how they were all happy at the end," Lisa said.

Marilyn then said to the class, "If I put one coin into the pot, how many coins could I take out of the doubling pot?" Hands shot up and

Marilyn asked the children to show with their fingers how many coins there would be. She scanned the class and saw that all of the children were showing two fingers. Marilyn recorded on the board:

$$1 + 1 = 2$$

"And if I put the two coins that came out back into the doubling pot, how many would there be?" Marilyn asked. The children each held up four fingers. Marilyn added a new sentence to the board:

$$1 + 1 = 2$$
$$2 + 2 = 4$$

"And if I put those four coins back into the doubling pot, how many would there be?" Marilyn asked. She scanned to check that all of the children were showing eight fingers. Marilyn added a third number sentence to her list:

$$1 + 1 = 2$$
$$2 + 2 = 4$$
$$4 + 4 = 8$$

"We don't have enough fingers for the next one," Alex said, anticipating Marilyn's next question.

Marilyn said, "You're right. This time, think about my question and raise a hand when you think you have the answer. If I put the eight coins that came out back into the doubling pot, how many coins would there be?" Most of the children raised their hands quickly; others needed to figure either by counting on their fingers or doing mental math. After a moment, Marilyn said, "Let's say the answer together in a whisper voice."

"Sixteen," the children whispered in unison. Marilyn recorded the new sentence on the board:

$$1 + 1 = 2$$
$$2 + 2 = 4$$
$$4 + 4 = 8$$
$$8 + 8 = 16$$

"Who can explain how to figure out that eight plus eight adds up to sixteen?" Marilyn asked. She called on several children to explain in turn.

Beau said, "You count on like this—nine, ten, eleven, twelve, thirteen, fourteen, fifteen, sixteen." He used his fingers to keep track of counting on eight numbers.

Janie said, "I just know it."

Ramon said, "I made a ten. I took two from the eight and put it on the other eight. And then there are six more, and ten plus six is sixteen."

Daniel said, "I took five from each. Five and five are ten. Then I had three extras from the first eight and three extras from the other, so that's six more. So it's sixteen."

Marilyn had been working with the students on addition strategies and, as she typically did, she recorded each of the students' methods on the board:

Count on: *8 . . . 9, 10, 11, 12, 13, 14, 15, 16*
Remember.
Make a 10:   *8 + 2 = 10*
               8 − 2 = 6
               10 + 6 = 16
Make a 10:   *5 + 5 = 10*
               8 − 5 = 3
               10 + 3 + 3 = 16

"I know how much sixteen and sixteen makes," Alex said, again anticipating the next question.

"Let's all think about that," Marilyn said. "If I put sixteen coins into the doubling pot, how many coins would there be? Raise your hand when you think you know." To make the problem clear, Marilyn wrote on the board:

$$16 + 16$$

As before, after giving them time to think and when more than half of the children had raised their hands, Marilyn had the children respond together in a whisper voice. She heard several answers in addition to the correct answer of thirty-two. Two girls explained.

Monica said, "Ten and ten makes twenty. And six and six makes twelve. So you take the ten from the twelve and put it on the twenty to make thirty. There are two more, so it's thirty-two."

Darcy said, "I imagine the numbers one on top of the other. Then I add six and six and put down the two and carry the one. Then I do one plus one plus one. It's thirty-two, like Monica said."

Marilyn continued this same routine for doubling, next asking the children to double thirty-two and then sixty-four and writing each problem on the board as she presented it. Both of these were easier for the children since they didn't involve regrouping. Now the list on the board looked like this:

$$1 + 1 = 2$$
$$2 + 2 = 4$$
$$4 + 4 = 8$$
$$8 + 8 = 16$$
$$16 + 16 = 32$$
$$32 + 32 = 64$$
$$64 + 64 = 128$$

Marilyn then presented the students with the problem they were to solve. "If we start by putting just one coin into the doubling pot, and then keep putting back the coins we get from the pot, we go from one to two and then four, eight, sixteen, thirty-two, sixty-four, and one hundred twenty-eight." Marilyn pointed to the problems on the board as she said the numbers.

"We skipped over one hundred from sixty-four all the way to one hundred twenty-eight," Marilyn continued. "I wonder if it's possible to put a certain number of coins into the doubling pot so that we'd wind up with exactly one hundred coins. What do you think about that?" After a moment, about six students had their hands raised. Marilyn called on Elena.

"Fifty will work," she said. "If you double fifty, you get a hundred."

Hiroshi added, "Fifty plus fifty makes one hundred."

Marilyn wrote on the board:

$$50 + 50 = 100$$

She then asked, "Could we get to one hundred if we put the coins in more than one time?" Some children nodded, seeming to think that this was possible; some shook their heads "no"; some shrugged; some didn't react. Marilyn continued, "Remember, each time coins come out, you have to put all of them back into the pot so they double again. Try to solve this problem and see what other numbers of coins we could start with and wind up with exactly one hundred coins."

Marilyn distributed paper to the children and they all got to work. She circulated, observing the children as they worked. She had to re-state the problem for a few of the children, but soon everyone was involved. They spent almost half an hour working on the problem.

Some students tested a lot of numbers. Marilyn was pleased to see Jeanette, a student who had difficulty with numbers, diligently work away. By the end of the period, Jeanette had found that 50 and 25 worked and that 10, 2, 3, 30, and 35 didn't work. (See Figure 19–1.)

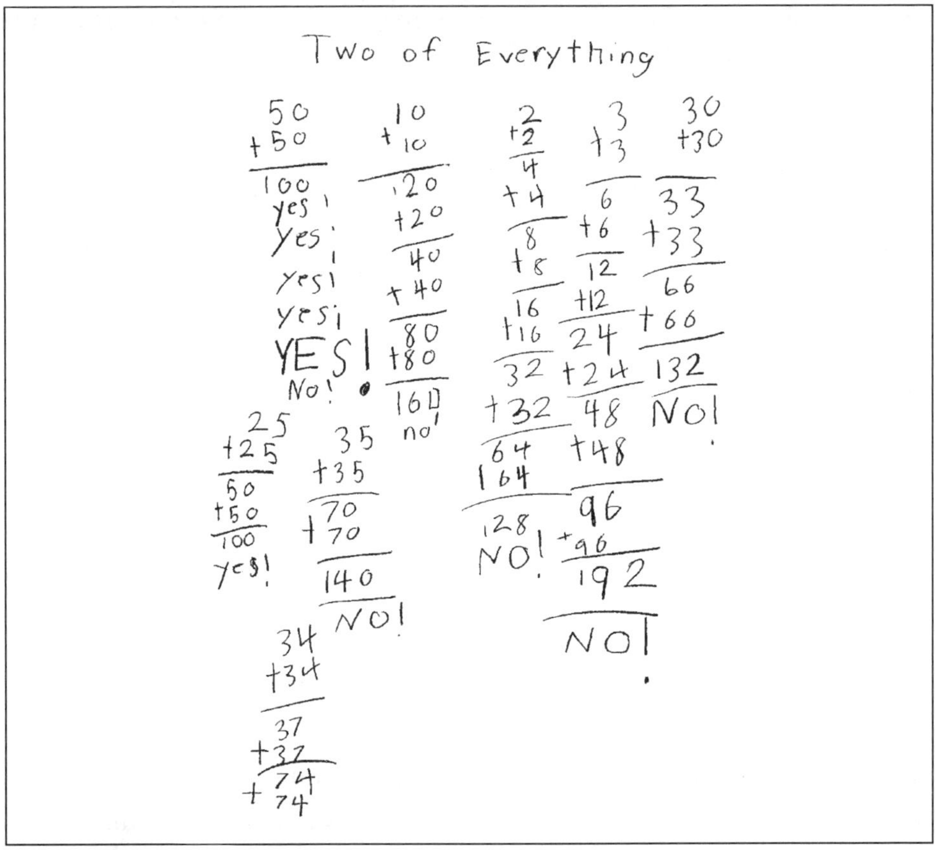

Figure 19–1: Jeanette tried several numbers and found that only fifty and twenty-five worked.

Sixteen of the children found that fifty and twenty-five worked; five recorded that fifty worked but couldn't find another solution; and two didn't focus on the problem but instead spent their time writing math sentences with expressions that were equivalent to one hundred. (These two students worked together and spent a good deal of their time writing everything twice—their names, the date, the title, and each problem. At least they understood what *twice* meant! See Figure 19–2.)

Most of the children who found fifty and twenty-five felt there were other solutions that they just couldn't find. Annette wrote: *There are more but they are to hard.* Her response was typical.

Eldon included one hundred as a solution. He wrote: *You take 100 and never put it in the pot.* Others liked his idea and added it to their papers.

Alex, who was fluent and confident with numbers, reported three solutions—one hundred (never put it in), fifty, and twenty-five. He wrote: *I think I have all the ways because you have to have $12\frac{1}{2}$ to make 25 in two.* (See Figure 19–3.)

Elena seemed satisfied that there were only two possibilities. (See Figure 19–4.)

The lesson was successful and the book became a classroom favorite.

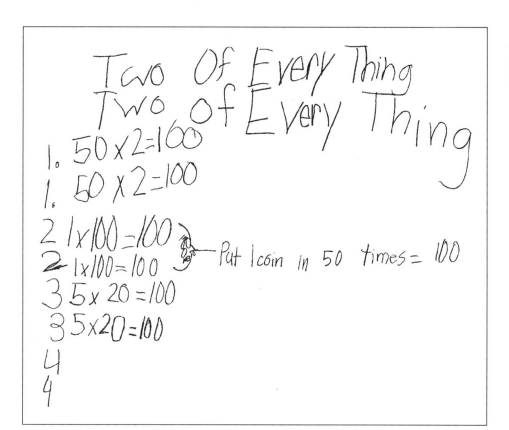

Figure 19–2: Monica got more involved with the *Two of Everything* theme than with the assigned problem.

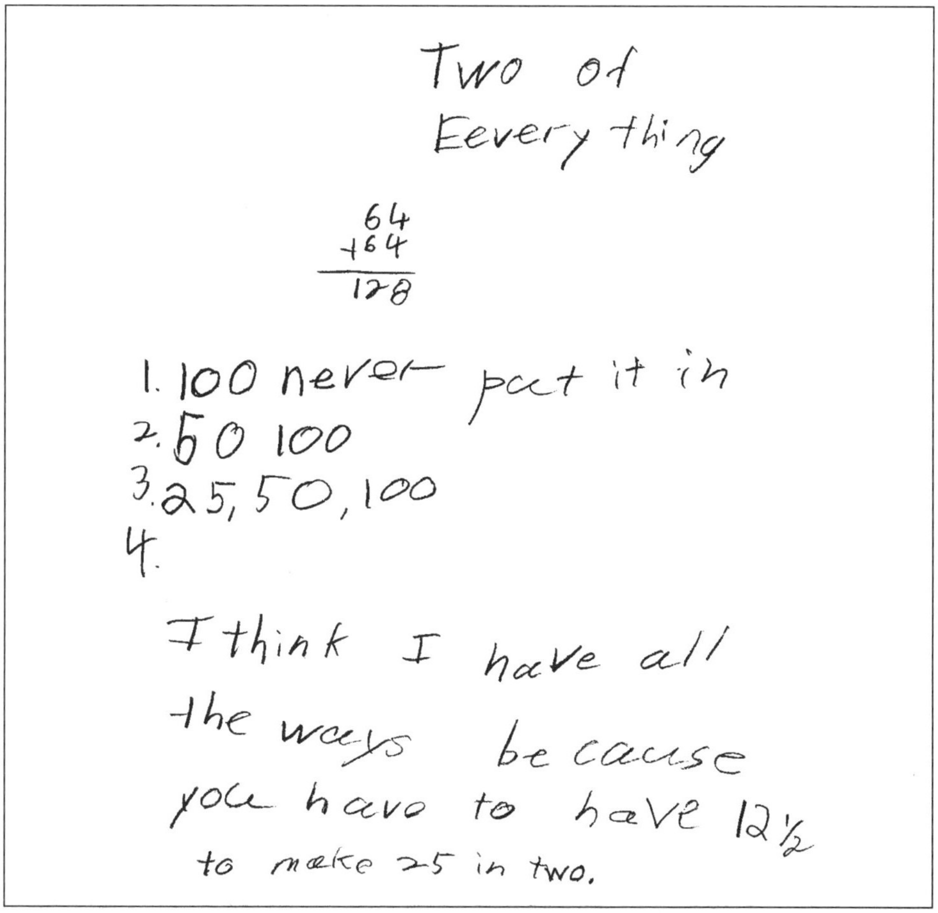

Two Of Every Thing
Two of Every Thing
1. 50 × 2 = 100
1. 50 × 2 = 100
2 1 × 100 = 100
2 1 × 100 = 100 — Put 1 coin in 50 times = 100
3 5 × 20 = 100
3 5 × 20 = 100
4
4

Figure 19–3: Alex used his understanding of halves to determine that twenty-five was the smallest number possible.

Two of
Eevery thing

$$\begin{array}{r} 64 \\ +64 \\ \hline 128 \end{array}$$

1. 100 never put it in
2. 50 100
3. 25, 50, 100
4.

I think I have all
the ways be cause
you have to have 12½
to make 25 in two.

Figure 19–4: Elena carefully illustrated her solution for putting in fifty coins, then used only numbers to show a second solution for starting with twenty-five coins.

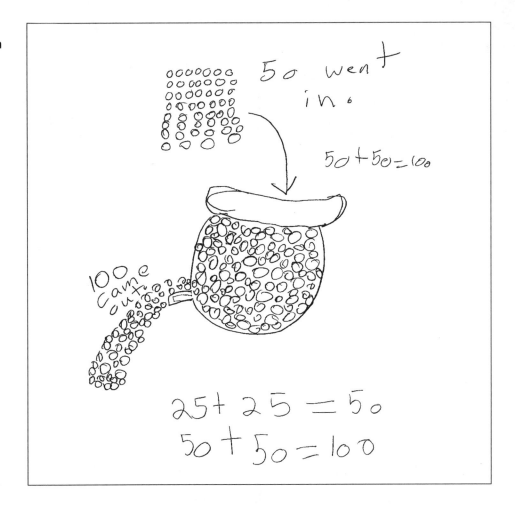

50 went in.

$50 + 50 = 100$

100 came out.

$25 + 25 = 50$
$50 + 50 = 100$

Two Ways to Count to Ten

Taught by Bonnie Tank

Two Ways to Count to Ten: A Liberian Folktale is retold by Ruby Dee (1990). The story promotes the idea that it's not always the biggest or strongest but sometimes the cleverest who wins the prize. The story is about the leopard's search for an animal to marry his daughter and rule the jungle after his death. Bonnie Tank read the book to a class of second graders and then involved the children in investigating number patterns.

MATERIALS

In *Two Ways to Count to Ten,* King Leopard gathers the animals of the jungle into a huge circle and explains how he will choose his successor. He flings his spear high into the air and says, "He who would be our prince must also throw the spear toward the sky. He must send it so high that he can count to ten before it comes down again."

The elephant steps forward to try first, but he fails. So does the bush ox, the chimpanzee, and the lion. Finally, the antelope succeeds. He flings the spear far up into the air, and before it returns to earth, he calls out five words: "Two! Four! Six! Eight! Ten!"

After reading the story to a class of second graders, Bonnie asked the children if they could think of any other ways to count to ten. Children had some suggestions. "Five, ten." "One, two, skip a few, ten." "Ten, like in ten, twenty, thirty." On the board, Bonnie listed the different ways to count to ten.

1, 2, 3, 4, 5, 6, 7, 8, 9, 10
2, 4, 6, 8, 10
5, 10
1, 2, *skip a few*, 10
10

She talked with the children about the number patterns and then asked, "What if the king had given the challenge of counting to twelve instead of ten?" As the children volunteered different ways to count to twelve, Bonnie recorded them on the board. She was surprised that some children were able to count by threes and fours, as she hadn't expected second graders to be able to do so.

1, 2, 3, 4, 5, 6, 7, 8, 9, 10, 11, 12
2, 4, 6, 8, 10, 12
1, 2, *skip a few*, 12
6, 12
3, 6, 9, 12
4, 8, 12

The children's interest was high, so Bonnie continued by having them think about different ways to count to fourteen.

Bonnie then posed a different problem. "The antelope won by counting by twos," she began, "but suppose the king picked a larger number. How would the antelope know whether counting by twos would work?"

In response, some children volunteered other numbers for which counting by twos would work. Bonnie listed their suggestions on the board and had the children test them aloud. Several children noticed that all the numbers they had listed were even.

"So the antelope would know that if the number was even, counting by twos would work," Bonnie concluded. It was then time for recess. On her way out, Cynthia came to Bonnie to explain her discovery. "I can count to nine by twos," she said. "One, three, five, seven, nine." So much for Bonnie's generalization!

A Follow-up Problem

Several days later, Bonnie returned to the investigation. She read the book aloud again, and the children were just as interested as they had been the first time.

"Suppose the king wanted to choose a harder number," Bonnie asked the class. "What number might he choose?"

One child suggested twenty and another suggested one hundred. "Let's try an in-between number," Bonnie said. "Let's figure out all the ways there are to count to forty-eight."

The children worked individually but consulted with each other. A few asked Bonnie for number charts, and she made 0–99 charts available to the entire class.

Children worked differently and displayed their work differently. Some listed the numbers they could count by while others also included numbers that didn't work. Some added or counted on their fingers to figure while others used the number charts to help. Some tested numbers in an orderly sequence while others experimented with numbers in random order. All the children were interested and involved. (See Figures 20–1 through 20–3.)

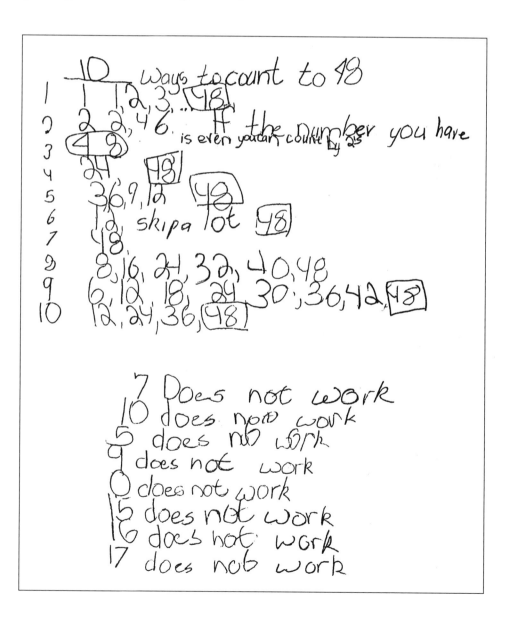

Figure 20–1: KC listed ten ways to count to forty-eight as well as eight numbers that he thought wouldn't work.

Figure 20–2: Eric listed the seven ways he found to count to forty-eight.

Ways to count to 48.
1. 1,2 skip a lot 48.
2. 1,2,3,4,5,6,7,8,9,10,11,12,13,14,15,16,17,18,19,20,21,22,23, 24,25,26,27,28,29,30,31,32,33,34 35,36 37,38,39,40,41,42,43, 44,45,46,47,48.
3. 2,4,6,8,10,12,14,16,18,20,22,24, 26,28,30,32,34,36,38,40, 42,44,46,48.
4. 8,16,24,32,40,48.
5. 6,12,18,24,30,36,42,48.
6. 4,8,12,16,20,24,28,32,36,40,44,48.
7. 48.

Figure 20–3: Maria described her reason for each of the nine ways she found to count to forty-eight.

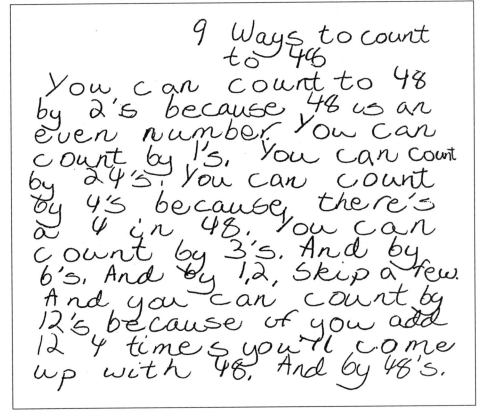

9 Ways to count to 48
You can count to 48 by 2's because 48 us an even number. You can count by 1's. You can count by 24's. You can count by 4's because there's a 4 in 48. You can count by 3's. And by 6's. And by 1,2, Skip a few. And you can count by 12's because of you add 12 4 times you'll come up with 48. And by 48's.

Blackline Master

A Cloak for the Dreamer Shapes

A Cloak for the Dreamer Shapes

References

Axelrod, Amy. 1994. *Pigs Will Be Pigs: Fun with Math and Money*. Illus. Sharon McGinley-Nally. New York: Simon and Schuster.

Burns, Marilyn. 1994. *The Greedy Triangle*. Illus. Gordon Silveria. New York: Scholastic.

———. 2001. *Teaching Arithmetic: Lessons for Introducing Multiplication, Grade 3*. Sausalito, CA: Math Solutions.

Confer, Chris. 1994. *Math by All Means: Geometry, Grades 1–2*. Sausalito, CA: Math Solutions.

Dee, Ruby. 1990. *Two Ways to Count to Ten: A Liberian Folktale*. Illus. Susan Meddaugh. New York: Henry Holt.

Fox, Mem. 1992. *Night Noises*. San Diego: Voyager.

Friedman, Aileen. 1994a. *A Cloak for the Dreamer*. Illus. Kim Howard. New York: Scholastic.

———. 1994b. *The King's Commissioners*. Illus. Susan Guevara. New York: Scholastic.

Geringer, Laura. 1985. *A Three Hat Day*. Illus. Arnold Lobel. New York: HarperCollins.

Goldstone, Bruce. 2001. *Ten Friends*. Illus. Heather Cahoon. New York: Henry Holt.

Harshman, Marc. 1993. *Only One*. Illus. Barbara Garrison. New York: Cobblehill.

Hong, Lily Toy. 1993. *Two of Everything*. Morton Grove, IL: Albert Whitman.

Lewis, Paul Owen. 1989. *P. Bear's New Year's Party*. Hillsboro, OR: Beyond Words.

Lionni, Leo. 1994. *Inch by Inch*. New York: Scholastic.

Losi, Carol A. 1997. *The 512 Ants on Sullivan Street*. Illus. Patrick Merrell. New York: Scholastic.

Moore, Inga. 1991. *Six Dinner Sid*. New York: Simon and Schuster Books for Young Readers.

Morozumi, Atsuko. 1990. *One Gorilla*. New York: Farrar, Straus and Giroux.

Myller, Rolf. 1962. *How Big Is a Foot?* New York: Dell.

Pinczes, Elinor J. 1993. *One Hundred Hungry Ants*. Illus. Bonnie MacKain. New York: Houghton Mifflin.

Rectanus, Cheryl. 1994. *Math by All Means: Geometry, Grades 3–4*. Sausalito, CA: Math Solutions.

Root, Phyllis. 2001. *One Duck Stuck*. Cambridge, MA: Candlewick.

Ross, Tony. 2003. *Centipede's 100 Shoes*. London: Andersen.

Slater, Teddy. 1996. *Stay in Line*. Illus. Gioia Piammenghi. New York: Scholastic.

Wickett, Maryann, and Marilyn Burns. 2002. *Teaching Arithmetic: Lessons for Introducing Place Value, Grade 2*. Sausalito, CA: Math Solutions.

Wilder, Laura Ingalls. 1932. *Little House in the Big Woods*. New York: Harper and Row.